Arthur Berm

When Reality Hits

From WW II to the New World Order

Produced by:

FriesenPress
Suite 300 – 852 Fort Street
Victoria, BC, Canada V8W 1H8

www.friesenpress.com

Distributed to the trade by The Ingram Book Company

When Reality Hits
By Arthur Berm

This story is about war and peace, about tragedies and triumphs, new beginnings and the good life that followed. Interspersed with humorous anecdotes and observations, the story continues, showing a slow deterioration and change in our society, general morality and that extreme ideologies and terrorism are becoming more commonplace, "Wars and rumors of wars" has Canada and America involved in conflicts around the world. It questions; is the UN failing as a peacekeeper? Who will bring peace and what is the answer?

Arthur is a happily married family man with two children, five grandchildren and four great grandchildren. Retired from a busy and varied business life is an avid sailor. As a Christian he felt the need to share his experiences and concerns for the future of our society and countries, hence the writing of "When reality hits."

"When Reality Hits" is available in 3 editions

Hardcover ISBN: 978-1-4602-3582-9
Paperback ISBN: 978-1-4602-3583-6
eBook ISBN: 978-1-4602-3584-3

"When Reality Hits" is available from:

Ingram Wholesale, Amazon.com - Barnes & Noble
Kindle Bookstore - Nook Bookstore
iTunes Bookstore - Google Books - Kobo Bookstore
FriesenPress Bookstore

Arthur Berm

E-Mail: Aberm@Telus.net
www.arthurberm.com

Table of Contents

Dedicated to my wife Irene for her continued support help, and encouragement in this project.

In memory of Kelly *"who lost in life but gained in death."*

INTRODUCTION

Growing up in Holland, Europe between 1940 and 1945 had its moments. Near the end of the Second World War, there was a lot of confusion. One day, a soldier started shooting at all the boys in my neighbourhood—just being a nasty individual as far as we could tell. Being not a very good marksman, he aimed at me but missed. Instead, he shot my playmate, a girl who was right beside me. Bertie was rushed to the emergency hospital, where they were able to save her leg. Later on, it became apparent that the soldiers had been given the order to eliminate all young boys to avoid future insurgents.

Once a week, my mother would visit my grandparents to make sure they were safe. On one such occasion, the German soldiers were stopping all traffic and confiscating bicycles, and any other mode of transportation. When mother saw that, she made an immediate U-turn. She started racing home, zigzagging down the road while the soldiers were shooting at her. When she reached home, she kept breathlessly repeating, "They can't have my bike; they can't have my bike ..."

Well my father, although relieved that she was safe, was furious at my mother. "That bike isn't worth your life! We can do without it, but we can't do without you!"

He was so right!

Another time when I was walking with mother, we were stopped by armed and uniformed goons who made us stand and watch, as some prisoners were forced to dig big holes, a lengthy procedure. When the holes were dug, we had to watch the prisoners being shot into the graves they had just dug for themselves. The next "volunteers" had to cover the graves. Afterwards, we were allowed to carry on with our journey.

History tells us that the Second World War came to an end during 1945, and that peace was restored. However, the effects and after-effects would be felt all over the world for many years to come, followed by the "Cold War." Conflicts in Indonesia and Korea would soon fill the newsreels and world peace seemed a long way off.

Living in Europe, and having survived the Second World War, I was busy with school and getting an education. For more than a decade though, the talk was often about warfare and atomic weaponry. This kind of talk made me want to shout: "Let me out of here!"

Thoughts about emigration were appealing and kept intensifying until I made the decision to go. My feelings about what war was like were being pushed aside by excitement about my move to change continents. A new location can change one's outlook on life. For me, it changed big time as the new country, culture, language, and friends re-shaped my life. Soon I became happier and healthier, but also more complacent. Memories don't go away; they just go to sleep, and are awakened as soon as something of a similar nature comes along. So I often say, "Oh that reminds me ..." and then bore some poor soul with my story.

When Reality Hits

Recently the political and economic events in Europe, the Middle East, and around the world (including the USA) have been intense. President Barack Obama being elected for a second term has made my concerns worse. The seriousness of the political and economic situation is shaping up to be a very big bang—and I certainly don't mean "The Big Bang Theory" ... far from it.

After reading Glenn Beck's book, Agenda 21,[1] my emotions were stirred. The book was written to bring awareness to what the United Nations' Agenda 21 might actually become. First presented in 1992, at the UN conference in Rio de Janeiro, Brazil, Agenda 21 considers the growing world population, resources, and a change in the behavioural patterns of people trying to cope with widespread hunger and poverty.

Having considered Glenn Beck's book as an interesting work of fiction, based on what the author gleaned from the *real* United Nations Agenda 21 document, and events I remembered from the past, I began to see certain patterns in the real changes that have been taking place in our countries. Looking at society's reaction to those changes, I felt the need to research the subject further. Recording what I found in my research became the reason for attempting to write about it.

When watching the news or listening to the radio, we are constantly bombarded with stories of terror, natural disasters, mass shootings, and terrorist attacks that often destroy so much and claim too many innocent lives. Often, much of what we see happening is set aside with a comment or question

---

1   Glenn Beck and Harriet Parke, AGENDA 21, New York, Threshold Editions/ Mercury Radio arts, a Division of Simon & Schuster, Inc. 2012

like, "What is the world coming to?" We may say, with some real concern, "We must make this a matter of prayer." But for myself, I know that (most of the time) these things are becoming too easy to forget, as we continue with our daily lives.

With all the changes that have taken place, and are continuing to do so, I'll try to give a clearer picture of what I see as *indications* of what is taking shape, both in the realm of politics and the economy, which affect both North America and elsewhere.

> "The world will not be destroyed by those who
> do evil, but by those who watch them without
> doing anything."
> ~Albert Einstein.

Thank you Mr. Albert Einstein, for bringing me back to a sense of reality and accountability, which is needed in the actions I take in my life.

1. Is my life under control?

When life is good, it's great. When the rhythm of a regular job harmonizes with life at home, life is good! When living in a comfortable home, near a good church, in a nice community, and working where appreciation and fairness are shown, life is great! With family life, social activities, and work under control, things couldn't be better. Oops. Without realizing, I used the term "under control." What I meant to say, was "under *my* control."

But it wasn't always like that.

Growing up in Europe, my life was anything but "under my control." Life, such as it was, had its limitations and they were affecting almost everyone. Working at a job was allowed at a young age. Starting at 14 years old, a youngster could earn a set wage, increasing each year per scale increments. Wages were set by a government agency, to a rate that could only vary slightly by area. There were no incentives for self-improvement, as there was no possible way to earn a self-supporting living until reaching 21 years of age—thus most (if not all) teenagers and young adults were left dependent on parents or family. So it was the parents who provided the incentives: "Go to night school and learn enough to support yourself!" Can you blame them?

This kept the population under some control, but it didn't end there because housing was kept out of reach. Most young couples, while earning a living wage, would be living with parents. Some of my friends spent several years on waiting lists for apartments. For the average young man, that living wage would only come after a compulsory stint in military service, where part of the training was learning to live on thirty-five cents a day—not even enough for a pack of cigarettes or a bottle of Coca-Cola. This type of training can be good, and military training has had a very positive impact on many young men in need of personal discipline. Military training is an important element of a country's overall defence structure, and important for the wellbeing of its citizens.

Ahhh … growing up and all the changes that come with it.

Looking back, I loved visiting my grandparents, who lived in another city reasonably close by. My grandparents owned a very nice home in a great area. They were privileged. When either Grandpa or Grandma had a birthday, the place would be buzzing with celebrating family members and friends. It would be almost like a national holiday. The garden, bursting with colours and scents, was always a lovely setting in which we youngsters could play and enjoy the goodies that were served in the gazebo. There was a pond with a little island one could access via a bridge; it had a plum tree, and was a delightful place to play and explore.

To us, the children in the family, everything was wonderful … but was it?

Both sets of grandparents had survived the First and the Second World War, but not without it taking a toll on their lives. It was the same story for many elderly people all around us; it was sad to see. The war had touched everyone to some extent—my family included. My cousin and a friend had both been taken to Germany as young teenagers, to a work camp, and were branded by the SS.

They were made to strip jewellery and other valuables from the bodies of Jewish victims—even their gold teeth had to be removed. My cousin survived physically, but he could never get over those horrible experiences. After several suicide attempts, he was finally kidnapped into the French Foreign Legion, where he served for many years. When he finally got out, he married a French lady and they started a small, but successful, restaurant business. He died after only five years of freedom.

When my grandfather died, the local authorities made my grandmother give up more than half of her home, so that a police detective and his wife could move into it and occupy the other part. Her housekeeper had to move out, because there was not enough room left for living quarters for her, and so her work was reduced. This was not a voluntary move for my grandmother; she also did not get proper compensation for losing the use of half of her house. Obviously, ownership of a home (and the rights that entailed) had lost out to the local housing authority's power and control. Was this the redistribution of wealth ideology creeping into our conservative country? How and why did we lose control? Did it start with apathy or was it simply that war?

Staying alive and healthy was a full-time job for many people, and it required a certain skill, and an ingenious approach to many daily tasks.

There had been frequent 'razzias' German raids, where going from home to home the soldiers would take able-bodied men prisoner to be shipped to work camps in Germany. Those were not pleasant surprises when they came knocking on the doors and certainly not considered welcome visitors.

One particular day stands out in my mind, there was a loud banging on the front door, mother answered by opening the door. Immediately there was some commotion as this German officer started coming up the stairs shouting that he was coming to take father away, "If you take one more step I will kick you right down" mother shouted at him, he backed off and took his soldiers with him; they left all together and we were safe. My mother, protecting us and my father who was sick and in bed, was our hero but this incident could have turned out differently and cost her life as well as our lives. We were blessed and protected from what could have been much worse, Some of the neighbours were not so fortunate and disappeared, one in particular Mr. Spykhoven came home after the war was over but he never survived very well, after a long struggle his health gave out and he died a broken man.

Fear is a powerful emotion as mother proved that day.

There was a group of patriots who formed what was known as the "underground" movement. It was not a social club or society and there were no complicated records or organizational structures; most people only knew one or two others that were directly involved. When information was needed it was mostly on a "need to know basis."

My father was heavily involved with the underground. He operated a secret radio station out of our home. With this, he kept news from the outside world coming in, and news updates from home going out to a command centre in England. This was a risky business, as the German radio truck was often patrolling, trying to find where those signals were coming from. Sending the messages was done at random times, some in code and always short. Fortunately, our radio equipment was never found by the enemy.

On one occasion, my father and his friend Pavoord were commissioned to sabotage the V2 installation, located not too far from our home. V1 and V2 rockets were first and second-generation guided missiles. Pavoord was an electronic genius, and at the cutting edge of technology at the time. At night, the two of them broke into the installation and realigned the guidance systems to send the self-propelled V2s back to Germany, instead of to England. Somewhere in Germany, the surprise arrival of the next few V2 rockets was a great victory for my father and his friend.

My Aunt Marge was a nurse like her two sisters, fully qualified and adventurous. Before the war she did some private nursing in Austria, in an undisclosed location, nursing and caring for a Russian Princess. The Russian lady reportedly was Princess Anastasia, daughter of the Tsar of the house of Romanov that were murdered during the Russian revolution.

When Aunt Marge's assignment was completed she came back home and became matron of a Hospital, resuming her life in the health care world of hospitals. Then the war broke out and life again took on some serious twists for her, she too became involved in the underground movement, just like my father.

The hospital had a large psychiatric ward and Aunt Marge used that to hide many Jewish women. She told them that it was extremely important that the German soldiers, coming to inspect, would be convinced that they were patients. Their lives and that of others depended on it. Apparently when the soldiers came, they did act very convincingly. She hid a lot of others too but sadly paid for it with her life. In the nineteen sixties the Jewish Government officials honoured her posthumously for her tremendous lifesaving efforts.

On the weekends we often would go visit my father's parents, Grandpa and Grandma, they lived in a nice part of Rotterdam called Chairlois; we would go by bicycle as no private automobile traffic was permitted on the weekends. The bicycles were fitted with child seats and my parents would make the journey a time of talking and singing and pointing out items of interest.

At my grandparents we would enjoy a time of visiting, often with other family members as well and playing in the garden where the Koi in Grandpa's pond were always fun to watch. The pond had a little island with a plum tree on it and Grandpa had built a drawbridge to the island, oh all so inviting. Wouldn't you know it I had to try and catch a Koi fish and fall into the pond although I seem to remember my cousin Piet helping a bit. Fortunately there were grownups nearby to pick me up out of the water before it became a serious problem.

Life is full of surprises and one night after a lot of commotion I met my uncle Jan for the first time; apparently he had escaped from German custody and came applying for political asylum at my parents' home. Under the cover of night darkness (there was a total blackout in force) he had made it to our area of town just ahead of his pursuers, the shooting and yelling alerted my parents to his approach and the loud knocking on the door of his arrival. Uncle Jan was somewhat short with his request for a visit that night but my parents did successfully hide him long enough to save his life. The house still has the evidence of the events of that night as a bullet gone wild left a hole still visible in the brick wall of the house.

My father's youngest brother Uncle Cor had an automobile business, which comprised a taxi service, service garage and a parking garage. It was a good business and provided much needed services in the South of Rotterdam. Part of the garage building backed onto a bakery and they shared a common wall, this part of the building came under close scrutiny. One day an officer of the German group who parked and had their vehicles serviced in the garage asked about the wall. Some light came shining through a new portion of the wall and this was a reason for their asking my uncle what was behind that portion of the wall. Quite some time earlier in the war he had his newest car stored and built in behind a new wall, unfortunately the ceiling light had been left on and could not be isolated. Uncle Cor just said the light is from the bakery next door …. they never found the car.

Doing business during the war years wasn't easy for most and my family was no exception. Uncle Cor was getting an increasing amount of traffic from the military vehicles through his garage, which meant a decrease in paying customers. One evening some large trucks pulled in for overnight parking, ever alert and vigilant, Uncle Cor checked the cargo which the trucks were carrying. The trucks were loaded with canned chicken destined for the Eastern Front (another project the German group was involved in) The cans looked very familiar

At the first checkpoint the papers were inspected, everything went fine and we could proceed, but when we got closer to the asylum there was another checkpoint and they wanted to see the patient, so Grandma found out what was going on; she lost her cool and actually looked quite convincing as being a patient, again we could proceed.

By now the German soldiers looked like nice friendly guys and Grandma like the enemy.

After a brief visit with Grandpa's acquaintance we were on the way back and the farmer was pleased to see us as arranged, Grandma cooled off when the produce was in the trunk of the car. With the papers in order we had no problems returning at the checkpoints; the driver could deliver us safely home......*yep that was my grandpa!*

Grandpa had a lot of spunk and when the occasion arose to solve a problem he always found a way. When playing games like dominoes he would cheat just to tease Grandma or anyone else that would be playing for fun, but if there were a thunderstorm he would demand everyone to be quiet because "GOD is speaking" he would tell us and he was very reverent.

In the rose garden Grandpa would show us how to pick roses without getting hurt and in his office he always had some fine Cedar cigar boxes for us to keep our treasures in, when people talked about smoking cigars he would say, "self preservation, smoked meat lasts longer" hmmm... I still remember the fine aroma of Karel 1 and Agio.

Our home was at the edge of town and we had a commanding view of the surrounding area, the house was built high on a sea-dike, we could see a small city some eleven kilometers away. When the air raid sirens would begin to wail and the drone of the airplanes filled the sky, we had front row seats to the Air show.

On one such occasion we watched the planes being shot at from the anti-aircraft artillery on the ground; several parachutes had opened up and the soldiers coming down, hanging on their parachutes, were easy targets now being shot at. Once on the ground, there was no place to hide in the open fields. The German soldiers rushed into the fields to take any survivors prisoner, coming up from the fields they had a few.

By now a lot of people had come to watch and as they were climbing up the dike, the Americans who survived being shot down were cheered on. There was a vehicle waiting to take the prisoners away, there were German soldiers and officers ushering them to the trucks. Then as one German officer was starting to get into the truck, a large American prisoner grabbed him by the scruff of his neck, put the officer behind him and said in a very loud voice "Americans first" then got in the truck himself. The applause was loud and long, but I'm sorry that he may not have survived that defiant act.

While out playing one day, we saw the "windmill" go up in flames, for some reason it was just after we had been watching some planes do acrobatics or dog fights as they are also called sometimes. This caused a problem as this windmill was used to pump water into the canals from a local ditch system and losing that windmill meant a large area of meadows now became flooded. Later the windmill was partially rebuilt into an electric pump station.

Somehow one of my parents had acquired parts of a kaki uniform from an Allied forces officer, a real prized possession,

The celebrations went on night after night, dancing in the streets around bonfires, singing and stories being told about other areas that were now set free. On one such evening a strange event occurred while the talking and singing was loud and boisterous, gunshots rang out, and suddenly a German military vehicle appeared, chased by a Canadian vehicle. The first vehicle ran right through our bonfire narrowly missing the partying citizens and the second vehicle followed closely also missing every one. Somewhat in shock but unharmed, someone started the singing again, another stoked up the fire and soon the festivities resumed.

The war was over, but the effects would be felt long after. Within a few years, my heartbroken grandmother died, and shortly after her, my father also passed away. We were left to face this cruel society without them!

My first job was in the Engineering Department of the company to which my father had dedicated his life; he had died in his office. Now I was right there, where he had worked so hard for so many years, surviving the war years only to die shortly thereafter. My sister was now working there also. The work was interesting and I learned a lot about engineering as part of my continuing education.

Our company had been awarded a government project that consisted of designing and building equipment for a number of minesweepers, 32 in all. Satisfied with our work, we were awarded another contract, for a branch of the military that commissioned our company to design floating (sea) mines. Everything was quite secretive, and the work was interesting, but it bothered me that our designs, of very destructive pieces of equipment, would be used to destroy ... and likely to kill. This made me change my mind about my work.

Most of Europe was struggling to recover from the Second World War which had left massive areas in ruin. Rebuilding was an enormous task.

In school and at home we learned that the Marshall Plan was designed "to rebuild war-devastated regions, remove trade barriers , modernize industry, and make Europe prosperous again.[2]" With the help of the Marshall plan, the oppressor's country was nicely rebuilt. Many of the smaller areas, without much industry, didn't get the same treatment. This was a little like what we see today, when a crime is committed against a citizen, the victimized citizen is left holding the bag, while the convicted criminal is being coddled by the authorities.

President Franklin Roosevelt, in his first inaugural address, said:

"The only one thing we have to fear is fear itself."

Fear can be a very effective tool, often used by those who are trying to intimidate. The worries about "Big brother" were very real, and we became intimidated by authorities that arrested people who had been gathering in small groups. Any more than three people gathering in conversation on the street were in danger of harassment, or worse yet, arrest. That intended intimidation, and the fear of being overheard by someone who may use it against me, is a feeling that has

---

2   Marshall Plan-Wikipedia, the free encyclopedia, http://en.wikipedia.org/wiki/marshall_plan/ (accessed February 5, 2014)

never completely left me. Now I'm wondering ... is this same thing going to be a problem here. Now?

Is "big brother" making a comeback?

Is he that guy I'm not sure about?

What's going on?

Work. Well finding work was never a problem. Everyone I knew worked, or attended school, and there always was work ... or so it seemed. Soon I started work in the shipyard, and continued on with my education—working the practical side of engineering. We were very busy most times, and no one complained about that, but when the work slowed down and there was nothing to do for days, I would hear complaints.

Again, restless and uneasy about many things that were happening, I could not settle down. The threat of nuclear warfare had remained, since the end of the Second World War, and the images of the nuclear attacks on Japan were still very fresh in my mind.

Another job was advertised and appealed to me; it could be considered a new direction in career. My application, by mail, was considered, and I received a reply by mail with a date and time for a personal interview. When I asked for a day of my holiday time, I had to give the reason, which was a normal request. I was denied the time off, because I was going to an interview for a new job! My heart sunk to new depths. So much for being honest —I felt betrayed. What to do?

As the day of my appointment came nearer, a plan had come together; at work we had nothing to do but waste time, so I snuck out and climbed over the fence, travelling by train to my appointment. Everything went well, and I was offered the job verbally — later to be confirmed by mail. Excited, I returned to the shipyard and climbed the fence to get in, talked to my fellow workers, and finished off the day.

When I received the written confirmation of the new job offer, I wrote a letter giving notice at my existing job. The notice to end my employment was not accepted by the company. Instead, I was summoned to a Labour Court.

Right to work YES, but right to change jobs NO.

At the Labour Court, the company claimed that I could not have gone for an interview, because I had been at work that day. Besides, the job was no improvement for me. Then I was allowed to explain my side of the story. I told them that I had applied for time off to go for an interview and had been denied. Then I explained that I had climbed the fence to go for the interview, and told them what the new job was about. Then we had to wait for the court's decision, which to my surprise, was in my favour. My letter giving notice at my existing job was accepted by the court, and stood from the day of my resignation.

My new job was great. I worked in a research and development laboratory for an optical company, where I was assigned to work on the development of a special vertical shutter system that would operate on a special camera with a 360 degree lens. This special camera was to be for military use. The next project was a shutter mechanism for a high-altitude camera for the air force—again, somehow the military popped up in my life, and my work.

Earlier I mentioned military service, of which it was such a privilege for young men to be a part. Well I got a formal invitation to join. When the day came for me to go through the physical and mental testing, I prepared myself for the event. I would choose the navy for my 18-month minimum term of service. The testing went fine—after all, I was a healthy, breathing, young man who was able to stand up and spell my own name.

My request to serve in the navy was denied. I was assigned to the air force, and privileged to receive officer training because of my education, which meant I would be serving a minimum of 24 months.

Now what did I have under my control?

From time to time, I had talked with my family about emigration. They had brought it up, and I had eagerly joined in and agreed that we would go. Now the idea of emigration was no longer an option. It had become a must, and immediate action was required.

Soon I asked to speak with an officer, so that I could explain my situation. An interview was granted and I explained that I was preparing for emigration. Spending the next 24 months in the air force would be a waste of taxpayers' money, and hard on my widowed mother as she would be forced to support me. The officer said that this was the first time he had heard emigration used as an excuse to get out of serving your country, but said that he would run it by his superiors.

When I heard from him again, he was smiling and told me that they were giving me six weeks to leave the country. I was delighted that they had accepted my request and would let me go. I packed up my personal stuff and headed home as a civilian, a very happy civilian.

An appointment at the Canadian Immigration Office was quickly arranged, and soon I was going through all the necessary steps: a physical exam, aptitude test, and confirmation of my education. Wouldn't you know it I didn't pass the medical exam. Hey what is going on, they just said that I was healthy enough to serve in the Air Force. Apparently there was a cloudy area over my lungs which they interpreted as TB so I had to run tests at the TB clinic; this involved going to the clinic several times a week for four weeks. The culture tests turned out to be negative and I was given a clean bill of health. As it so happened I had been nursing a bad cold when the medical testing for the Canadian Embassy was done. Then came my acceptance, and the job of making arrangements for travel. It had taken a lot longer than what I had hoped for but I just made it!

One day after the six weeks were up, the Military Police came to my home, saying that they would like to speak to me. Smiling at them all the while, my mother said, "So would I, but he left the country yesterday." By then I was somewhere in Greenland, waiting for repairs on my airplane, which had experienced engine problems. Some time later, we made it safely to our destination, Quebec City and after some days, our final destination, Vancouver, British Columbia. Final destination was maybe "wishful thinking" considering the many moves that lay ahead.

My freedom came at a cost, which I didn't want to acknowledge until much later. For now, I thought I had things mostly under my control.

My new life started in a new country, speaking a new language, and making new friends. I was becoming part of a different culture, and was filled with so much excitement that

I was in my element. Nobody here was talking about what I had to do or what I did wrong.

Meeting people came easily, and one day I met Chris Qualheim, an interesting fellow from Norway who had just sent his wife back to Norway—apparently homesick. Chris told me that he was going to work for a timber company, making big bucks working on Vancouver Island before going back to Norway to join his wife. He didn't have to twist my arm too much before I gave in, and agreed to come along. The work was with the Tahsis Lumber Company. The day we left Vancouver was a beautiful, sunny spring day, making our trip from downtown Vancouver to downtown Nanaimo a terrific experience. The bus ride from Nanaimo to the Town of Campbell River was also very nice. In Campbell River, we were picked up by a company representative and taken to Gold River Camp.

Camp was a big place that was really more like a small community. There were bunk houses, a large dining hall, a big cook shack, a very large boiler room, some houses, and an office building.

On arrival, we got a brief indoctrination session and were assigned a to a small house that was set up with bunks. This would be our home from then on. Breakfast for the first shift was at 5:30, and we were told to report for work early in the morning—really early, as the crummies (personnel carriers) would leave at 6:00 a.m. for various locations in the woods.

After getting settled in, Chris and I walked around the camp to become familiar with our new surroundings. The camp was situated at the head of Muchalat Inlet. There was a mechanical workshop and garage for equipment repair close to the log dump, at the river estuary. We discovered that, as part of the camp, there was also an activity centre and a company store. Next to the camp was a small Indian reservation. To our knowledge, Sam's family were the only occupants of that reserve. Sam worked for the Tahsis Logging Company. Later on we got to know Sam and his family, and how they lived. It had been a full day travelling from Vancouver to Gold River. Packed with new impressions and experiences, we knew that the next day would come early—real early!

Those early breakfasts were the best. There was no limit to all the terrific food, and of course, new and intriguing items to try out. There was one item I just could not bring myself to try though: something that looked like boiled onions, lots and lots of them, being served in big bowls for breakfast. One day at breakfast, someone asked me to pass the bowl of figs to him. Boing! A light went on. These "onions" were delicious figs! I had not yet enjoyed them thinking that they were boiled onions. Dumbo!

The work we had hired on for was "setting chokers" in the Steel Spar high-rig operations, which were popular at that time. Where we would be working, the trees had already been cut down. Our job would be to tie heavy steel cables around the logs. Those cables were in turn tied to a long overhead line, which would then lift and pull the logs to a landing area. The whole show was run by the "rigger," a foreman who would watch our every move from a distant vantage point. He would give signals to his sidekick, the "whistle punk", who in turn would blow a horn with the code signals from the rigger. If done correctly, it was a very efficient and safe method for that time.

We had an English fellow as our whistle punk—a nice young man, but not quite right for the job. Nicknamed "Preacher", he was the first British logger I had ever encountered. He would read on the job. Sometimes he would be slow to respond with the signals, but one day he started blowing the wrong signals altogether, while Chris and I were still working with the cables. We were almost buried under tons of logs. After digging out and being checked over we continued our work till the end of the workday.

Preacher was run off the job by our rigger in an unprecedented manner, and a message was sent around all the logging operations on the coast, telling them not to hire preacher as a worker in the woods.

Our curiosity about the Indian reserve, and Sam, would soon be satisfied. Travelling on the company crummies provided an opportunity to meet other workers—not so much during the early hours on the way out to the sites, but rather on the way back to camp. After meeting Sam, he invited us over to meet his family. Sam's house was set back in the woods adjacent to the camp and the Muchalat inlet. We went in and met the family: his wife and two daughters. The house was not all that big, but pleasant, with modern appliances like a fridge, stove, and washing machine. Sam showed us that the fridge actually held extra blankets. "Why are you storing blankets in the fridge?"

"Well," he said sheepishly, "we have no electricity. The salesman in Campbell River never checked if we had everything necessary to run the appliances." They had no running water either.

The previous summer Sam's family had been in town and made another big purchase: a twenty-one-foot boat with two fifty-horse-power outboard motors, Sam had used the boat one time and his nets had been gobbled up by the outboard motors. He went back to his old, wooden, motor-less boat, and the new boat was left sitting where he abandoned it. Sam being the generous guy that he was, offered me both his daughter and the boat. It left me blushing and somewhat confused. "Hmmm, well, the boat sure, but the boat and the girl? You're too generous Sam."

Each year Sam would take his family on vacation as soon as the fire season started. Just like clockwork fire season came and we all left the camp to go to town or home, town for me was Campbell River. The next day I saw Sam's wife and I asked her "When are you leaving for San Francisco?" "Oh we do this every year," she said, and "When we get to town Sam has to have a beer but it never stops with one and then we never make it to San Francisco, but it's alright, I'm used to it."

An accident can spoil your whole day, and after an unfortunate and painful fall it spoiled more than my day. The work in the woods requires that the men wear spiked boots in order to get traction when walking on logs. Properly equipped with my boots and hardhat I was able to walk and run on logs that were down. After awhile I started to feel free to run and jump from log to log. The day I fell I was rushing to do my work and as I jumped from one log and landed on the next, the bark broke loose from the log and sent me flying backwards, legs up and back down, landing on the first log, fracturing my spine in several places. I was taken to a hospital where I was treated.

The limited treatment I received in the Campbell River hospital was rather shameful. Unfortunately, I remember precious little about what happened after the accident, my hospital stay, or returning to camp. This was my first experience with a Canadian hospital. I don't know how long I was there, but soon, rather than keeping me in the hospital, I was returned to camp and was put on light duty. Perhaps this was the Workers' Compensation Board's way of cutting costs? My excuse is, I had no knowledge of Workers' Compensation Boards and their purpose, but being a new Canadian, I had to learn the hard way.

My days were filled with getting treatment from the camp medic, resting on the first-aid room beds, and listening to the dispatcher in an adjacent office. Later on, some dispatch duties were added to my daily routine until the medic released me for regular work again. The camp medic was an interesting character. He was one of the BC Lions' Football team medics but it wasn't a fulltime job for him so he doubled as camp medic for us. Not being too familiar with the football team and their extra staff at the time, I must have disappointed him by my lack of interest in his important position.

Many years later, it was discovered from new X-rays that my spine had been seriously fractured in three different places, and fortunately, by my taking care of things, it had healed well enough to let me live a relatively normal life—my taking care of things were the operative words there.

The work in the forest turned out to be hard, tiring, healthy, challenging, exciting, a great learning experience, and I loved it. In a short time, I became the assistant forest engineer for the timber cruising and reforestation operation, and it proved to be an interesting job.

2. Learning about "Apathy"

As our daily life settles into a certain routine, and we take our life seriously, it can also become somewhat boring. In fact, it's possible to get totally side-tracked. Yes, I hear you; I see your lips moving, but I don't take in what you're saying. When that happens, we often unknowingly look at diversions, not aware that some of the changes that could affect us are actually even taking place. This condition is often referred to as *Apathy.*

My new start in life, in this new country, began fine. There was work to be had, and friends to make. All around, it seemed like this new beginning was just what I needed. Sure, I made some mistakes (as I believe we all do) but there appeared to be a much kinder, gentler, more relaxed attitude all around me. I could make a good living by working hard. It turned out to be a good life. After living in a couple of boarding houses for a while, I rented a bachelor apartment, which was as nice as I had ever seen. I could afford it and still live well.

It was around this time that there was much talk about Cuba and a fellow called Fidel Castro. He had the idea the Cubans didn't really know what they wanted so he would help them by imposing his type of ideology on them. Obviously, still confused about the issue, the Cubans didn't all agree with brother Fidel, and he had to help them some more by forcing his ideas on them. This caused some hard feelings and Fidel had to resort to stronger persuasion. This reduced the Cuban population somewhat and Cuba has never been the same!

Sorry for interrupting myself but if I don't do it my wife will, anyway. It took me a while before I caught on to the fact that there were many nationalities represented in my new world, and to my surprise and pleasure, it was very easy to connect with most people—to share and learn from them. One of the nationalities that intrigued me most was the Canadian, and by that I mean the aboriginal Canadian Indian. Still mostly living on reserves, they were the people I had read about, and heard about as a fearless, proud, distinct group, with skills unknown to most other nations. Needing friends and friendships, I started seeking them out to learn from them, but found a lot of beaten, disappointed, and discouraged people. There were some outstanding people, of course, like Chief Dan George, Len Marchant, and many others who worked tirelessly for the improvement of the Indian life and public image, and many others who have, over time, brought back dignity and respect to the various tribes and individual members—people like Angus Heathen, my Plains Cree friend, and his son Kenny, and Johnny Kanapatetuw, who taught me about hunting and many customs of the Cree Nations. Then there was the Partridge family—no, not the TV Partridge Family—and their native art. The Cree Partridge family made us understand how treaty life on the reserve had affected their generation. The friendships I shared with all of them will always be treasured.

There was so much to enjoy and learn about customs and practices. I enjoyed a lot of help from my friend Johnny. He would come by with his wife, Dora, for a visit, and each time would tell me another story. The Plains Cree Indians have many customs that are very interesting. One of those customs is that people share everything with each other. Another one, as Johnny told it, was that if I liked something and told him that I liked it, he would give it to me—plain and simple. The next time he came over was just after I had been hunting. I was cleaning my rifle. Looking at it carefully, he said to me, "You know I really like that rifle." A little later, he again said, "Yeah man, I really like that rifle." Now I had to respond to him, so I said, "Okay John, you can have my rifle, but I do really like your truck. In fact, I love your truck!"

Quickly, he handed my rifle back to me, and said "You learn fast, really ... too fast!" We both had a good laugh.

In Holland, I was used to working forty-eight-hour work-weeks, now with a normal forty-hour workweek, with full two-day weekends, I had lots of time for myself. I was over-joyed that the beach, which I loved, was close by. Still, some-thing was missing, you say? Well not really, I met a lot of girls at a church youth group, and now—at my apartment—my neighbours were two Scottish girls! Mmmm. The Scottish people are well known for their thrifty approach to life, this was something I had learned firsthand, they lived up to their reputation.

One evening there was a knock on my door, they had been told that I worked for the telephone company and wondered if I could come around to perhaps fix their phone. Now I must tell you, I did work for the telephone company, but in the engineering department, I had never fixed a telephone in my life. That didn't seem to bother them at all, they had me trapped. Not one to be defeated easily I took the handset and unscrewed the speaker part of the phone, pulled it apart and quickly blew in it a few times, put it back together and voila! the phone worked fine. It occurred to me that the phone had been working all along and I fell for it.

One thing led to another and I invited them for a meal, soon the deal with them was simple: one night I would cook for them, and they cooked for me the next night. It was an ideal set-up for the Scottish girls, who got a two for one meal deal all the time and they lived with the notion that I wouldn't catch on. They really thought that they had out-smarted me!! Well I must tell you, it would take at least three of them to out-smart me, being Dutch.

To step into the future for a moment, I want to mention that we had some good times, indeed. Spending many happy hours at the beach with them, I fell in love with one of them, and then married her. She has been my wife ever since, and we recently celebrated our fifty-second wedding anniversary.

But I must get back to my story, dealing with the everyday life of an average, hard-working young schmuck—like I was back in the day. All was going well with us. We had a house, a mortgage, a dog, a cat, and one and three quarter kids. I drove or took the bus to work, carrying a bagged lunch. The wife had a station wagon to drive the kids (no longer fractional) around, to pick up the shopping and attend to a number of household chores.

When I was a bachelor my shirts and slacks were attended to by the drycleaners, now my wife took on those chores for which I should have been grateful. My wife didn't mind ironing my shirts however to save time and electricity she would only iron a small part on the front of my shirt that was visible when I had my jacket on, oh scotty! She did a lot better with my slacks; she could press a razor sharp pleat, however they would look much better and less embarrassing when the pleats are to the front and back, not to the left and the right! As they say we got all that ironed out fairly soon and she became an even greater wife.

Hey what happened, my shirts and my slacks aren't getting pressed any more?

One day when she was doing the washing, she took my jeans and put them into the machine, after the washing cycle was complete, she wondered what had caused the thumping noise. Looking into the washing machine there was my Big Ben pocket watch on the bottom. Although the spin cycle had removed some of the water, the recovery process was not yet complete, so armed with the Scottish book of household hints, Irene preheated the oven and proceeded to dry-out my watch. The heat from the baking process was effective enough to melt various less durable parts of my watch, Oh boy!

It can be interesting how some things work out at times; we had seen a place for sale and were very interested in buying it so we went to meet the owner. It was a nice day and perfect for a motorcycle ride, so we approached the place from an adjacent road and took a run at the embankment of the property. We were expected to arrive but not in this fashion. We climbed the embankment and cleared some air before stopping in front of the gentleman with the open mouth. It impressed him so much that he wanted the motorbike as part payment of our new home.

Now that we had a home we had to have a dog and soon 'Gypsy' filled that position. Can you believe it that little puppy, so cute and cuddly, soon turned out to be a big dog, much like a cross between a Border Collie and a German Shepard. We had to build a home for her so she could have some privacy when she needed to be alone. The doghouse turned out to be a bit of a strange place, Gypsy would not go in it if we were around but as soon as we were gone she would be the resident queen. Playful as most young dogs are, I had sprayed her with the garden hose at times while I was out watering the grass. Having left the garden hose out for use next day I was surprised to find the chewed-off end of the hose, but the spray nozzle was nowhere to be found and guilty looking Gypsy went into hiding.

Sometimes the "keeping up with Jones" syndrome sneaks into our lives. Gypsy's house seemed a little plain and I got an idea to redecorate her house. To give it a more established and rustic look, I mounted a nice set of Moose antlers on the front of her house. Proud of the improvement to her mansion I brought Gypsy out to look and appreciate my work of love. To my surprise she acted strangely, whimpering first, then growling at the antlers and backing away. But the antlers, the Moose no longer attached, didn't react, so the dog went into the attack mode by barking and charging at the antlers. Still no reaction from the Moose antlers: she'll get used to it we said.

Some days later we were inside enjoying a well-deserved cup of coffee, we could hear Gypsy barking at the imaginary intruder, when all of a sudden there was this loud yelp and then some cries and whimpering. Being the responsible parents that we were we rushed out to investigate, there was our baby Gypsy in pain and the offending antlers, half hanging down and half on the ground. The dog's constant physical attacks had dislodged the antlers which in defense had returned an attack by falling on poor Gypsy. Oh poor baby! We totally removed the antlers to avoid further attacks on poor Gypsy.

This lifestyle had us going comfortably along, year after year, with the kids growing up, and everyone getting older, including the cat, dog, and our circle of friends. We just didn't seem to even notice how quickly the years were going by.

Really, I wonder how we, as people, can be so busy being comfortable and living the good life that we don't feel guilty about our passive behaviour, and for neglecting to defend our true beliefs. Well, I suppose we all just like our way of life, and as long as we do our part, just don't see the problems around us as clearly as we should. We hear about unemployment, for example, and the painful situations that it creates—even making people lose their homes—but unless it affects our immediate family or circle of friends, it doesn't feel much like a reality.

While we are busy with our daily lives, we're rapidly approaching a time when our lives will change dramatically, into a completely different and unknown existence. Our lives will no longer be our own, and because so many have lived their lives in apathy, not paying attention to or having seen many of the warning signs, will be unable to return to our former lifestyles.

During the years of living my own comfortable life with my family, a lot of things were happening—changes that sort of escaped us at the time. There it is again, that apathy thing. They're just little things we lost mind you, but over time, they became many little things ... and now we've lost a whole pile of them—little things that can eventually affect our freedom.

It reminds me of my friend Gerry's little son. Every evening, as they walked past our home, the little fellow would take up some gravel (from our driveway) in his little hand and walk home with his dad. At the end of summer, there was a small bald area in our driveway, devoid of gravel. Had this been allowed to continue on for some years, the gravel of our driveway would have covered Gerry's driveway, and his little son could claim to have redistributed the wealth—our gravel.

These are some of the little things that come to mind— signs of how things can change without really being noticed— like the stores and pubs being open on Sundays, liquor stores being privatized, and smoking being banned in public places. If you're lucky the mailman *might* stop at your house a few times per week—none of this morning and afternoon mail anymore.

Laws were passed that you must wear a helmet when riding a motorcycle, and when driving in a car, you must be strapped in with seat belts; little children need to be strapped in special car seats. More recently, new drivers are on probation for a year or more, and no one is allowed to use their cellphone while driving. Of course, while these are changes that sort of snuck up on us, they are, at least, for our own health and safety.

It also seemed strange to have to buy a fishing license to go fishing in the salt chuck, even for crabs, or needing a license to go out in your boat. Even hunting licenses have changed; you don't just buy the tags now, instead there are lotteries to win tags for certain species. People are even getting fined for watering their lawns too much.

Where were we when these changes happened? These little things ... changes that sort of snuck in to alter what was familiar to us? Were we asleep?

Going on a date used to mean taking a girl for dinner and a movie. As far as I understand, nowadays a date usually ends up in sex. Maybe that's a reason for the high number of rapes.

Traditionally, Friday nights were family shopping nights, with the whole family out shopping for whatever was needed, and this was considered by many as an entertainment night. For many families, a snack at A&W or Dairy Queen would wrap up that night out.

Do you ever wonder what a hamburger and fries will cost when the school kids working at McDonald's get unionized? Their prices have already been going up lately, but soon it will be impossible to see any sense in going for an inexpensive burger at the Golden Arches. This applies to most fast-food restaurants, and there are enough of them. Of course, when the profit margin goes down, the prices go up or the product decreases in quality or quantity, and sometimes both. In North Seattle, we used to eat at a restaurant on Aurora that served an unbelievable burger with real grilled meat, a nice slice of ham, and all the trimmings. Mmmmm!!!!

When we were in Seattle recently we went looking for that 'special burger' treat but the restaurant was no longer there, replaced by some other business!

Today a variety of fast food restaurants cater to the needs of many people—not so much to families, but rather to individuals on the run, school kids who do not carry lunches to school, and friends meeting for a bite to eat and a visit. For many people it's an almost daily routine.

Some changes went :

from:	to:
Right to work	- if the UNION lets you
Right to bear arms	- gun control / no guns
Fast food treat	- fast food diet
Sacked lunches	- restaurant lunches
Marriage and family	- single parent or common law
Single car family	- multiple cars per household

(My friends have two drivers in the family and five vehicles.)

The family unit was once a very strong part of our society, but that too has changed. More marriages are of a short duration. Single parents are all around us, and many couples never get married for fear of commitment or failure. Attendance at churches is down, and many new and less-known religions and sects are appearing all around us. We've all heard about how people are searching for the truth, and we can see that they are often searching in the wrong places. But what have we done about it?

In the mid-sixties, I met Richard Wurmbrand and his wife, Sabina. Richard was a Christian pastor in Romania who was imprisoned for his faith. He was incarcerated twice, and Sabina was imprisoned once. Richard spent eight and a half years in prison the first time, and about five years of a twenty-five-year sentence the second time. Then he was given his freedom through an amnesty. When talking about his faith and imprisonment, Richard would have praise for his Saviour and pray for his jailors and torturers. At first though, he was very upset about the North American Christians, and their apathy regarding those tortured for Christ.

The Wurmbrands' concern for those Christians being persecuted for their faith never left them, and they worked tirelessly to help the Christians in communist countries. This concern led to the founding of "Jesus to the Communist world".

As the ministry spread beyond the communist countries, the organization became known as "The Voice of the Martyrs".

The many years of being incarcerated and tortured by the communist regime because of his faith, did not kill his burning desire to tell others about his Saviour; it never waned but kept growing. This was a selfless and positive act by the Romanian pastor, his wife and their son to take it upon themselves to help others imprisoned for their faith and inspired more people to join them in forming the organization.

Don't live with apathy in your life.

3. Keeping the Peace

The last century started off with a bang with the the First World War. Archie Bunker might have called it *"double yuh double yuh one"*, but regardless of what you call it, war is war, and not a very nice way to start a new century. This big war made quite an impact everywhere, but especially in Europe, and it just made sense to look for a way to avoid repeating it.

The First World War (WW1 1914 — 1918) made many aware of the terrible losses, death, and destruction wars can cause. Various governments (even from countries outside of Europe) received urgent requests, and demands, that this should never happen again. Hence the League of Nations was born.

The League of Nations

A group representing various countries met at Versailles and agreed on an alliance to form the League of Nations. It came into force January 10th 1920. First 42 countries joined the

League of Nations, and later another 15 countries joined.[3] [4]

Because of modern technology, like radios and telephones, governments could communicate effectively, without having to rely on courier pigeons for urgent news. Cross-border and farther international interaction was making it possible to work together.

Along with the quest for peace came economic and social progress. Tourism was making a strong comeback, and with it the smuggling of certain goods. My grandmother and aunt were in their glory, with the thrill of travel and smuggling!

The League of Nations had two primary functions:

First — keeping peace among the member nations through a council for arbitration and conciliation, which would hear any dispute between member nations and seek a resolution.

Second — promoting cooperation between member nations' economic and social affairs.

As recovery from the First World War continued, and the various economic and social affairs began to unravel, a new problem appeared on the horizon: The Great Depression.

The Great Depression was felt in varying degrees all around the world. Europe got its fair share of it. This was just the precursor to the next big world event: the Second World War. It

3   Franklin, Access to the FDR Library's Digital Collections,Www.FDRlibrary. marist.edu/archives/collections/franklin/ (accessed Jan. 28 2013)

4   League of Nations — Wikipedia, the free encyclopedia, http://en. Wikipedia..org./wiki/league_of_nations/ (accessed Jan. 13 2013).

was immediately clear that the League of Nations had failed in keeping the peace. The League had no military power of its own; it depended on its member nations, and they were not willing to use sanctions—economic or military.

The United States never joined the League, and Germany, the USSR, Japan, and Italy all withdrew in time. The League depended mainly on Britain and France. It was difficult for the remaining governments, long accustomed to operating independently, to work through this new organization.

The United Nations

During the Second World War, leaders of Britain, China, the USA and the USSR, started talks about forming a post-war organization. In 1944, representatives of Britain, China, the USA, and the USSR met at Dumbarton Oaks in Washington, DC, where they continued their talks and laid the foundation for an international organization.

In 1945, representatives of 50 countries gathered in San Francisco, between April and June, preparing the final text that would become a basis for the United Nations. The original United Nations had 51 member countries. [5]

By 1946 the League of Nations was no longer, but most of its ideals (and some of its structure) were kept by the United Nations. The ideals of peace, and social and economic progress remained the basic foundation (and goal) of this new Global organization.

---

5   United Nations, Wikipedia,the free encyclopedia, http://en.wikipedia.org/ wiki/united_nation/ (accessed Jan. 13 2013)

The UN took steps to form a Security Council from the League's Council. Five permanent members—Britain, China, France, the USA, and the USSR—were also given veto power, which meant that decisions taken by the Security Council could be blocked by any of the five permanent members. There are ten other countries who each serve two years terms on the Security Council. The Security Council is the principle UN branch responsible for ensuring peace. It is also the only body whose decisions are binding on all member states.

For me personally, the formation and establishment of the UN was exciting. I felt a sense of security, especially when my friend (after serving in the navy) came home with a large silver medal for having served in Korea on a peacekeeping mission.

Since the creation of the UN, the balance of the big powers has changed, and now over one hundred new member states, mainly non-western, have joined. With these changes have come increasing demands to reform the Security Council.

Preventing war and peacekeeping is no small task, and as many more nations joined the ranks of member countries at the UN, other problems popped up. Racism and repression begged for attention. The Charter of Rights had to be included in the UN charter, as well as many other sorts of things of that nature, such as the Universal Declaration of Human Rights.

The peacekeeping duties alone are not enough for the UN, and the organization is looking into other areas that could be added to the work of the UN—areas that are staring the various members of the group in the face: poverty and illness. There are poor and sick in *every* nation, even outside the UN member nations ... actually, *especially* outside the UN member countries.

Growing up has a lot of challenges for the average individual, and I must admit that I really was no different. The war was over in Europe, and although we were free, there was the constant reminder all around us of what warfare can do to a society and to our lives. With those reminders, it wasn't too surprising that an organization to prevent another war had tremendous appeal.

We were led to believe that the purpose of the United Nations was to bring all member nations of the UN together to work for peace and development, based on the principles of justice, human dignity, and the well-being of all people, allowing the countries to share in national interests and work together to solve international problems.

There are currently 193 members of the United Nations. They meet in the General Assembly, which is the closest thing we yet have to a world parliament.

We are told that the United Nations is supposed to be a centre for helping nations achieve and keep the peace throughout the world, to develop friendly relations between nations, to work together to help people live better lives, to eliminate poverty, disease, and illiteracy in the world, and to encourage respect for each other's rights and freedoms. All Member States have sovereign equality. All Member States must obey the Charter and nations must try to settle their differences by peaceful means. Member nations must avoid using force, or threatening to use force. The UN *may not interfere* in the domestic affairs of any nations. All member nations are encouraged to try to assist the United Nations.

Oh yeah, I remember 1945, and thinking that we were safe now that we had the United Nations taking care of business.

Most of Europe was faced with rebuilding, from the damage inflicted by the Second World War. You can't rebuild something unless it's broken down, can you? Well, broken it was: buildings, infrastructures, economies, and lives. The old timers who had survived the First World War had had to go through it all again.

How on earth could the British soldiers march and sing "Oh, oh, oh, it's a lovely war."[6]

In 1945, the ballpoint pen made its debut; the stores started selling them and we soon heard that the pens would wreck our handwriting skills. At first, they were not allowed in the schools, and Crown pens survived for several more years. The Fountain pen would never be replaced of course. Television was up and coming technology, and in 1945 there were nine TV stations serving less than 7000 working TV sets in the USA.

In 1947, Bell Laboratories developed the first transistor, and in 1954, the first transistor radio was produced. They gained immediate popularity, and by the 1960s and 70s, billions had been produced. The changes that the transistor brought to the world were mind boggling. For instance radios had been using glass tubes that were power hungry items, keeping radios from being really portable, because of the lack of 110-Volt power sources. The transistor meant that a radio could now be small and light, without the glass tubes, and run off a low-voltage battery, making it both portable and affordable. Transistorized ignition in cars became a great improvement as

---

6   Lyrics from "Oh! It's a lovely war." J.P. Long and Maurice Scott, 1917

well. Transistor and hard-wiring technology changed a lot in the industry.

During the United Nations' Conference on International Organization, in April 1945, references to health were incorporated into the United Nations' Charter, and it passed a declaration that an international health body would be set up.

To see what the real intent of the UN was, let's look at what followed its establishment. In 1946, the Economic and Social Council of the UN helped organize the World Health Organization (WHO). The use of the word *"World"*, rather than *"International,"* clearly showed what the UN had (and still has) in mind.

WHO is another UN branch. Not to be confused with The Who, the 1960s rock band, Who, a.k.a. the World Health Organization, is a specialized agency of the United Nations, focusing on international public health. Its current priorities include communicable diseases, HIV/AIDS, malaria, and tuberculosis in particular.

The organization publishes the World Health Report, the Worldwide World Health Survey, and other reports. Its links with the International Atomic Energy Agency, and its distribution of contraceptives, have both proved controversial ... and no the controversy has nothing to do with glow in the dark contraceptives.

For a number of years, my boss ("Doc Stanley") served as a member of the Expert Advisory Committee on Environmental Health for the World Health Organization. His involvement with the WHO provided some work, and didn't hurt our Consulting Engineering business at all. We designed and built water collection, water treatment and distribution systems as well as sewage collection, sewage treatment and disposal systems for cities in developing and war torn countries, including Vietnam and Belize.

The 1950s brought another big step in the field of communications, and by 1952 there were 20 million functioning television sets in the USA. The following year, colour television broadcasting began, and by 1965, the colour television industry was booming. Here comes the next war, with all its gore and bloody misery, in living colour!!

The Treaty of Brussels

How could anyone in Europe forget what had caused so much suffering and devastation? And now the USSR, together with several other communist countries would push their idealism on others in Europe. This concern led to the Treaty of Brussels in 1948, by Belgium, the Netherlands, Luxembourg, France, and the United Kingdom, which later formed the NATO Agreement.

North Atlantic Treaty Organization

In 1949, another organization was formed to keep the spread of communism at bay. The North Atlantic Treaty Organization (NATO) is a military alliance based on the North Atlantic Treaty, which was formed in 1949. The member countries, as an organization, agreed to protect each other in case of attack from any enemy. [7]

Ah yes ... April 1949. I had just purchased my second ballpoint pen. I was considering giving up my Crown pen nibs,

---

[7]   NATO — Wikipedia, the free encyclopedia,http://en.wikipedia.org/wiki/ NATO (accessed Jan. 13 2013)

since there was no real evidence that the ballpoint pen was destroying my handwriting (it remained as bad as always). I secretly wondered if some of the NATO Treaty documents might have been signed with ballpoint pens.

NATO's headquarters is in Brussels—the pride of Belgium. The total military spending of all NATO members makes up more than 70 per cent of the world's overall defence spending. In 1949, the first Secretary General was appointed to NATO. Lord Ismay proudly assumed the position and proceeded to say that NATO's aim should be "to keep the Russians out, the Americans in, and the Germans down." [8]

As an organization, NATO seemed nothing more than a political alliance at first. The Korean War changed all that. NATO's participation pulled the member countries together and strengthened its military structure as well. At just six years old, NATO was facing the Cold War. Russia and the communist nations formed an alliance and signed a mutual defence treaty that came to be known as the Warsaw Pact. This was perceived as an anti-NATO movement, designed to spread communism farther into the rest of Europe.

As with most organizations, NATO was not perfect. Along with doubts about NATO's defensive abilities against a possible Soviet invasion, the relationship between the European countries and the United States of America also had its ups and downs. This led to the development of the independent French nuclear deterrent, and the French withdrawal from NATO's military structure in 1966.

---

8   NATO — Wikipedia, the free encyclopedia,http://en.wikipedia.org/wiki/ NATO (accessed Jan.13 2013)

All of Europe was on pins and needles for some time, but gradually things settled down. Although the threat was very real, the dreaded atomic war that Russia had threatened never happened.

President Ronald Reagan, during a 1987 visit to Berlin, said:

"General Secretary Gorbachev, if you seek peace, if you seek prosperity for the Soviet Union and Eastern Europe, if you seek liberalization, come here to this gate! Mr. Gorbachev, open this gate. Mr. Gorbachev, tear down this wall!"[9]

My son is an avid runner, and has taken part in some popular events, including the Boston Marathon. While on assignment filming a documentary about the wall and life in East Germany, he ran on the wall for exercise, to the amazement of the East German guards. They watched him closely, but never stopped him from doing his runs; after he would have some gifts for them as a gesture of friendship. Some years later, after the wall had come down, James presented me with a piece of the wall. He had chipped it out, had it mounted on a walnut base, and added a little inscription about the date and place.

So, the Berlin Wall came down in 1989, and after that, NATO became involved in Yugoslavia. NATO's first military involvement was in Bosnia (from 1992 to 1995) and later in Yugoslavia (in 1999). NATO began to seek better political

---

9   Tear down this wall! -Wikipedia, the free encyclopedia, http://en.wikipedia. org/wiki/tear_down_this_wall/ (accessed Feb. 10 2013)

relations with former Cold War rivals, and this allowed several former Warsaw Pact states to join NATO in 1999 and 2004. [10]

The member nations of NATO had agreed that an armed attack against any one of them, in Europe or North America, would be considered an attack against them all. They all agreed that, if an armed attack occurred, each of them would assist the member nation being attacked in restoring and maintaining the security of the North Atlantic area.

Three airline planes started out on regular line flights but turned into terrorist missions early on September 11, 2001. The terrorists forcefully took over the planes and diverted from the original flight plans to do their dirty work and commit horrible crimes using the airplanes as deadly weapons. They attacked the World Trade Center in New York, and the Pentagon, causing great loss of life and destruction. A fourth plane, also commandeered by terrorists did not reach its intended target but crashed in a field, killing all aboard. The terrorist attacks took more than three thousand innocent lives. Those attacks were the only occasion in NATO's history that could be seen as an assault on *all* NATO members. After the attacks, troops were deployed to go after Mr. Terrorist himself, Osama Bin Laden, who was hiding in Afghanistan.

Let's hope that the Taliban will be reduced in strength far enough so that the Afghan forces will be able to keep control in the country without a Taliban or Al Qaeda insurgence creating another repressive situation. Too many lives, too much

---

10 Ronald Reagan Presidential Foundation & Library; NATO — Wikipedia, the free encyclopedia, http://en.wikipedia.org/wiki/NATO (accessed Feb. 10 2013)

bloodshed, and too much effort has been spent by foreign and domestic military forces in Afghanistan to see the return of Taliban rule ... or Al-Qaeda influence.

There appears to be a real problem, with too many agencies—the UN, NATO, ISAF (as well as each country involved with restoring the peace)—involved in making decisions, but none willing to take full responsibility in all the peace keeping ventures.

Too many cooks spoil the broth.

If you are like most people you must
want peace, really want peace!

4. Life versus Euthanasia

Life is sacred. The right to live or die has long been a topic of discussion, and most nations consider the taking of a person's life to be an unlawful act. Getting to live a long, healthy, and productive life is not guaranteed, but even when sickness and disease strike an individual down, it is no reason for euthanasia. Assisted suicide, in the case of someone living with an incurable, very painful disease, or in a vegetative state, has been before various courts, and in many cases turned down— it is generally considered an act of murder.

We consider life to be sacred, and it is. We keep murderers alive on death row for many years. Often, when even mass murderers are convicted of terrible crimes, we keep them alive, look after, and even protect them. So why are we hearing that the United Nations favours euthanasia for the elderly? Are the elderly more of a burden than murdering criminals, who are being catered to full time? Why do we tolerate that nonsense?

Many times lately, I have been amazed at what medical science has accomplished. It seems advances are being made in the medical field. More and more, we are seeing the elderly reaching ages in excess of one hundred years, as a result of knowledgeable doctors and modern medicine. What must be confusing and frustrating for doctors, whose Hippocratic

Oath requires them to preserve life, is having to face requests for euthanasia. This could change the Hippocratic to the hypocritical.

To be honest I'm not proud of the Netherlands being the first to legalize euthanasia. The misuse of the practice is now at a source of alarm, some of the proponents, relatives, are sorry the laws were passed and abuse is happening. In 2011, an estimated 4500 deaths by this legal practice occurred; the exact numbers are difficult to report, as more than twenty percent is never reported. For those who pushed for that legislation, it must be difficult to deal with as second thoughts cannot change what has already been done.

Deep sedation is also on the rise in the Netherlands and prolonged or continuous deep sedation is to be considered as a type of slow euthanasia.

The UN proposes through the WHO to add euthanasia or assisted suicide into the right to health, and adding a new treaty on the *"rights of the elderly to end their own lives for the benefit of society.*[11]" [12]

There is a very definite danger of abusing this procedure and it would be hard to control.

Now doesn't this sound like population control? Sure the world population is growing, but traditionally wars have taken

---

11   U.N. proposes euthanasia as right to health (it was only a.., http://www.freerepublic.com/focus/f-news/2791827/posts/U.N.-proposes-euthanasia-as-right-to-health-(it-was-only-a-matter-of-time)/ (accessed Sept. 19 2012)

12   U.N. proposes euthanasia as right to health,http://OneNewsNow.com/culture/2011/10/11/un-proposes-euthanasia-as-right-to-health (accessed sept. 19 2012)

care of that. Hmm … of course war is what the WHO/UN is trying to prevent, although not too successfully.

Euthanasia, or painless killing to relieve suffering, has little to do with age, and to suggest that the elderly should take their own lives, to perhaps make room for someone younger, is an outrage! When discussing euthanasia, it was suggested that advanced age impacts the ability to exercise recognized rights, and that it is a case of patient autonomy to decide to end life. The idea is not being well received by those who respect life. My mother, a nurse by profession, was matron of a hospital for the chronically ill. As a teenager I would go visit with some of the patients and over time formed friendships with some of them. Personally, I cannot think of any of those people smart, intelligent and handicapped, being eliminated because of their condition or their age.

My mother would turn in her grave if she knew that Holland had legalized the practising of euthanasia. Now that I think of it, might she have been one of the victims herself?

If in fact the WHO/UN would be successful in adding euthanasia to the treaty then the elderly could be pressured by their children, doctor, or society, to end their own lives. But let's consider the fact that some of the most productive years of an individual's life is in their sixties and seventies. This raises the question of who decides at what age people become more of a burden than they are worth. We know there is no such thing as a fountain of youth, but we must be able to live our lives without being pushed out or thrown over the cliff!

Throw Momma From the Train was a funny movie, but lets not take it literally.

Is it the United Nations that decides our time is up? Is it one of the many countries that have gone (or are going) bankrupt because of wasteful spending? Is the next step for the New World Order—ooops, I mean the UN—to recommend euthanasia to anyone with a chronic disease? Obviously the UN doesn't consider life *sacred*. Are we really losing control over our right to live?

Some years ago, three whales were caught in the Arctic ice. Tremendous efforts were made to save those majestic mammals. Millions of dollars were spent, and there was great interest in the media to provide coverage of the rescue efforts.

At about the same time as the epic story of the whales was unfolding, there was also an article about a sick homeless man trying to enter a hospital. No assistance or media coverage was provided for him, and after hours waiting, he died right on the hospital steps. This story was reported too, and made an obscure appearance on the local newspaper's last page.

Obviously, those whales were not homeless, just lost in the Arctic and in need of international attention and help.

Are we becoming too casual or careless about life?

As part of an Engineering consultant's job comes the responsibility of considering safety and potential dangers created by ideas and designs. Traffic fatalities may be a need for improvement of a traffic pattern or an intersection, for instance. When discussing repeated accidents at certain intersections we looked at what would warrant installing traffic control lights. One of the criteria was the number of fatalities that had occurred at that location. This procedure had to place a price on each death, the death of a real person, an awful way of looking at the value of life. The cost of a traffic light equals four or five human lives, barbaric!

We know that the U.N was set up to keep the peace, and that they have gone beyond the call of duty on that account, but they are out of line when they begin to interfere with the domestic affairs of any country, and that includes justifying and encouraging euthanasia. Remember, one of the original rules of the UN: *"The UN may not interfere in the domestic affairs of any country."*

Again, our *apathy* has allowed some little things to slip by without our objections, and now we are faced with serious problems that must be resolved.

Euthanasia, as well as murder, are not acts that can be reversed. Such behaviour obviously can and will bring remorse for many, as whether by legal or other means, the taking of a life is easy. Bringing it back is impossible.

Euthanasia continues to be a moral and ethical problem that isn't going away any time soon!

The discussions about life versus euthanasia have gone on for a long time, and will surely continue for a long time to come, but my feeling is that the pro-life choice should not even be a choice. Euthanasia should not be an option. It is *not* an option. It is not at all a problem for the UN, as it must remain a national concern—NOT an international or global one.

For many, that discussion is a very painful problem. It is the problem that should be euthanized!

When we had our two kids, then our five grandkids and now our four great-grandkids, each brought joy, I consider how precious life is and every one of them so special. Yes, life is sacred, that never changes.

If you must choose, choose life!

5. To clone or not to clone, that's the question

Genetic engineering has been around for a long time, with good rewarding results, more recently though it has caused a lot of reason for concern.

When I think about genetic engineering, I think of Hawaii and the story of waste that went on in the canneries before the shape of fruit was changed. At the time pineapples could not be exported unless they were preserved in cans, as transport was taking too long and the fruit would spoil before it reached the consumer. One of the first altered fruits is the pineapple. Its original shape didn't lend itself to canning without a lot of waste, because in its natural shape it was roundish, and inconsistent. Fruit growers decided that their canneries would have to make an effort to be more efficient and less wasteful. To improve, they had agriculturists working on changing the shape of pineapples, to fit into round tin cans without a lot of waste, and hence the cylindrical shape of today's pineapple.

The use of genetic engineering in agriculture has given us a variety of fruits and vegetables that we now take for granted, but they are altered or relatively new. Take the average table grape, today they are almost always seedless. It wasn't always like that, they had lots of seeds inside the fruit. Although it is nice not to have the seeds to deal with, it must have been some process of sterilization to make them that way. I wonder if it is something that may also affect us.

"Genetic engineering is rapidly replacing traditional plant breeding programs and has become the mainstay of agricultural crop improvement."

Maurizio G. Paoletti[13]
Researcher, Department of Biology
University of Padova, Italy

Think of the human cloning possibilities. You get two identical people. They are interchangeable. It's like you have a spare. Well I've tried it. That can backfire. My friend and I, in the prime of our youth, had met the perfect dates. They were identical twins, and we had some fun double dating. The girls were fun to be with. They enjoyed a joke and so did we. Forget double dating now go into overdrive. This is great.

Things were going real well for a while ... until my date mentioned something personal that I knew I had never talked about with her. After dropping off the girls, I talked some with my friend Hans, only to find out that he'd had a similar experience. That's when we both realized that *they* were interchangeable, but we weren't! Those rascals!!

Human cloning is the creation of a genetically identical copy of a human, but not a natural born twin. Thus natural multiple births are not clones! Oh. Okay.

---

13 Genetic engineering in agriculture and the environment.., http://business.highbeam.com/411908/article-1g1-18826502/genetic-engineering-agriculture-and-environment-assessing (accessed Mar. 15 2013)

So does this mean that it would be possible to come across some genius that may clone his idol, maybe a modern Frankenstein or Dracula, scary possibilities? Just think, that next clone could even become a new Adolf Hitler or Joseph Stalin or Vladimir Putin, this is becoming nightmare material. Thoughts of human cloning possibilities are troubling me such as, imperfections, diseases, grotesque errors and devious minds could start showing up, this could conceivably get out of control, we don't need more problems. Is this where the Zombie movies came from, maybe some Zombie scriptwriter was hoping for a twin brother or sister by being cloned?

As mentioned before, the ethics of cloning is an extremely controversial issue. It also is a moral one. We are already faced with the moral issue of euthanasia. Man should neither take a life nor artificially create it.

For many years there has been speculation by scientists and policy makers about whether or not to take the prospect of artificial human cloning seriously. Cloning of mammals, although far from reliable, has reached the point where many scientists are knowledgeable. The literature is readily available, and the implementation of the technology is not very expensive compared to many other scientific processes.

Dolly, the cloned lamb was very much a lamb and had an amount of attention by the scientific world; this still does not solve the ethical problem of cloning.

Some think that by waiting until the first clone is among us, or about to be born, we complicate the problem. The UN may be concerned about losing control in the area of artificial human cloning. They like, and want to control, the cloning issue.

With the world population bursting at its seams, there should be an urgent suggestion from the UN for all the nations of the world to ban human cloning, except for medical research. The ban would also avoid having to prepare legal measures to protect clones from potential abuse, and discrimination. Slowing down the natural birthrate, through the use of contraceptives and education, is fine, but to then start artificial human cloning makes little or no sense.

Almost all governments oppose human cloning, and more than 50 have legislated a ban on it. But negotiations about an international ban collapsed in 2005, because of disagreements over research cloning, also known as therapeutic cloning.

As with euthanasia, the subject of artificial human cloning presents a variety of ethical and moral issues. The discussion by medical doctors and scientists around the world about artificial human cloning is far from over.

My hope is that artificial human cloning will be a subject that the government of each nation will take seriously, that they will be responsible and not allow it to be a UN responsibility.

Don't mess with life, it is too precious.

6. Education

The need for education starts early in life, and we learn a lot of useful information before we are even enrolled in an official school. For instance, I learned at an early age that metal knitting needles stuck into an electric wall outlet can give you an amazing boost, especially from 220 Volts. I stopped crawling immediately after that, and walked everywhere, quite energized, from there on in.

From an early age, we need guidance from our parents. School is also geared to provide guidance. Some teachers give more than others, but they all must do their part to shape our lives for the good of all. To some extent, we must cooperate with those who instruct us in the important things in life.

Wanting to be of help to my first grade teacher, I felt a need to introduce biology into our curriculum. So I brought a friend to meet my teacher and classmates. Freddie, my frog, was pleased to leave my pant pocket, but my teacher just screamed. It must have been with delight in seeing Freddie. Because of my good intentions, I was allowed to continue with my education ... I was going to say without any further incidents, but that would be stretching the truth a little.

As young boys we understood enough about the war that we had to help in the fight. Some of the older boys in the neighbourhood had a plan that would involve a number of us warriors. The plan was that we would remove ammunition from the German supplies and store it for safekeeping in the graveyard. This would cut out the middlemen or the 'intended victims'. The older boys would steal the ammunition under the cover of darkness and later we younger fellows transported it to the storage place. We carried load after load as if we were playing a game and by slipping through a fence, deposit our precious cargo in our hiding places.

With so much ammunition passing through our hands I started a collection of the various sizes and calibre of live shells that I kept under my bed. It was by all accounts a nice collection of some souvenirs with deadly purposes. One day my father called me to account for my activities, apparently Riet our maid had been trying to impress my mother by cleaning under my bed and she had discovered my cache. Now it was my father's turn to not be impressed with my actions. Very carefully and in detail he explained what I had done and that it could have caused some very unpleasant consequences. The next day most of my collection was disposed of in an appropriate manner without incident.

This episode left an impression on me that I have never forgotten.

After that I learned another lesson from my friend Rens who, also like me, had been involved in the ammo caper. He was curious about the reaction that heating these bullets from Germany would have; he took a handful of them and tossed them in the potbellied stove that was used to heat the room and also cook on. He didn't have to wait long for the results, the stove exploded promptly and left a chunk of cast iron embedded in his body. He quickly got to see the emergency hospital from the inside but lived to tell the story.

There must have been something about Rens and potbellied stoves because some time later a new stove had been delivered and was in place where the old one had met its final moments. As we were playing some game Rens said "let's light the stove and take the chill out of the air". We got some paper and stuff to burn, which we started immediately, however the silly thing had been put in place but was not hooked up and the chimney was plugged to keep the cold out.

It's amazing how quickly a smoking stove can get instant attention from the authorities, in this case Rens's mother; of course the flames may also have contributed to that.

We learned a lot back then and school added some of the boring stuff they said was not only necessary but the law. We must have learned a lot because there was the promise of graduation in the end that sounded important, graduating! Well I must admit that there was a certain feeling of being smart but something was missing. What we didn't have when I went to school was sex education, and now it's a little bit too late to teach me the subject. Besides, my teacher has since died.

Normal sex education is an instruction to issues relating to human sexuality and human sexual anatomy; sexual relations, abstinence (Wow, education has failed on this one!), birth control, and other aspects of human sexual behaviour—such as plain lust. Sex education should come from parents or caregivers and public health campaigns, but young kids often have their own ideas, and talk among themselves—keen to find out about the "birds and the bees."

Experience has shown that adolescents are curious about some (or all) aspects of their sexuality, as well as the nature of sexuality in general, and that many will wish to experience their own sexuality as soon as possible.

For many generations, discussion on sexual matters was considered taboo. In the past, sex education came from parents, and this was often put off until just before a youngster's marriage. Most of the information on sexual matters was obtained informally from friends and the media, and most of it was of little help, especially during the period following puberty when curiosity about sexual matters was the most acute. Sex education programs in schools were instituted, initially, over strong opposition from parent and religious groups.

Sex education *should* stand for protection, improvement, and development of the family, based on accepted ethical ideas.

Hellooo? Did you have any input into what was taught at the school your kids attend? I know we didn't. The curriculum was going to include sex education—take it or leave it!

Sex education or "sexuality education" involves education about all aspects of sexuality, including information about family planning, reproduction, and information about all aspects of one's sexuality, body image, sexual orientation, sexual pleasure, values, decision making, communication, dating, relationships, sexually transmitted diseases and how to avoid them, and birth control methods.

Well there you have it, and I missed all that, so now we know where I would fail if I had to go back to school. Oh oh ....

hold on, my wife figures I would have no problem passing sex education. I suppose she has some inside information.

Why is there teaching of in-depth sex education in grade school? No way is that needed before the kids are taught the basics, like how to spell, read, write, add, subtract, and divide! It won't even hurt to throw in some geography and social studies. It is too late to start learning these basics when pupils are allowed into university.

There have been more changes in the education system, and what happens (or doesn't happen) in our schools will have an effect on the future. Public prayer has been removed, and even banned from our schools. Big efforts were made by Madalyn Murray O'Haire (an American atheist) to remove prayer from the curriculum of American public schools. She was proud of her accomplishments.

So we get sex education. Fine, I missed that in school, but I got my share of it elsewhere and I've muddled along quite okay, thank you very much. But removing prayer from our public schools? Wow, that's bad!

Then there is the subject of "new math." I didn't mind helping my kids at night after school, but new math? Now part of the common curriculum, this new method of teaching math seems to cause more confusion for the kids than any-thing, and I was glad to show my kids the easier way—the old way.

"Hey Dad, now you've done it!"

The teacher wanted to know how they had arrived at the answers, and my kids showed him how they had done it. Well, even though the answers were correct, he didn't like it because it wasn't his way.

Naturally I was a bad parent, and could not help myself. I was critical of the system. And having been part of the educational system, I feel duly responsible ... oh yeah!

In the past I spent some years as a training consultant to Malaspina College, now VI University on Vancouver Island; also for a Management Consulting firm in Toronto, Ontario, developing training programs for various industries across North America.

We all know what it is like to be speechless, I assume, but to realize that a person cannot read or write is an experience that has left me speechless several times in my working life. When men were assigned to work with me on projects, to write material for training purposes, and I would find out that they were illiterate, it left me in shock. People in positions of leadership, or in charge of responsible procedures, must be able to communicate ... and that requires literacy. The amount of trickery and persuasion applied by those who are illiterate is amazing, I have also worked with some deaf and dumb people, which is another disability that makes life very difficult, but they can usually read and write and their handicap does not affect their intelligence or ability to learn.

There is no doubt in my mind that a person who is not able to read and write is severely handicapped, and in order to survive in daily life must work very hard to keep their disability secret from those they work and associate with.

In the past, when I've been faced with such a case, we quietly discussed it in private. I would offer an anonymous teaching session, and help them learn without others being aware of the situation. You may ask how this even happens; nowadays everybody goes to school, and yet somehow kids slip through the system. They become good in acting. They act knowledgeably, and learn how to avoid situations that may expose their lacking skills. Next comes the state of denial, where it is too embarrassing to admit illiteracy.

Most people in those situations have confidants who will keep the secret quite well, and are willing to write a report when asked or cover in some other way for their friend.

Going to eat, there are some things that are almost guaranteed to be on the menu of any restaurant, like hamburgers, BLTs, or tossed salads, and simply ordering them avoids potential embarrassment. Another trick is to look at what somewhat else is having at a table nearby, and say, "Hmm, that looks good; I think I'll have that." I'm sure it's hard work, yet the solution is so simple: just learn to read and write.

Here is another thing that I never understood: why did kids need to learn about mythology? If Christianity and the Bible are supposed to be based on a myth, how can we be taught mythology without teaching the "myth" about the Bible? Would that not be teaching an incomplete subject, or is it because the Bible is true, and not a myth?

But then, if the Bible is true it should be taught ... shouldn't it? Ooh you say, but they teach comparative religion in schools; this may be true but some of the text books on that subject have five or six pages on the Muslim religion, but Christianity and most other religions get only one page at best to explain how they compare.

Education in general has undergone tremendous changes, but it is not addressing the needs of society, industry, or the economy. It is shocking to have an engineer who cannot write a report without errors, or a teacher who cannot write an essay without spelling mistakes. Don't talk about doctors who can write legibly, because there aren't any. I'm sure they take courses in scribbling. Even more amazingly, there are those who do the drug dispensing who can actually read some of the doctors' writing. What about those who excelled in political science and are working at fast food restaurants, or the young man who has a degree in liberal arts and works in the local smoke shop?

Our local college turns out many hairdressers annually, far too many to supply jobs for, but even so it remains a course that attracts many students year after year. Yesterday I talked with a university student who was about to finish her several years of studies to become a teacher; she told me that an official from the education department of the government had addressed the students in her class. They were told that jobs would be difficult to get because there were too many students, for the few positions available, graduating each year.

There could be an opportunity with them, though, filling positions as career counsellors! Oh ... you mean they don't have courses for career counsellors?

Sometimes I think that education is too important to leave to strangers, and when it comes to driver education, I must admit that I'm a pretty good instructor. We had some friends who lived in a rural area, and so when we visited them, it seemed like a good opportunity to start my wife's driving lessons. After all the preliminaries of my instructions, Irene seemed quite confident that she could handle it. We were on a long stretch of straight road in a quiet area, and so along we went. Then it happened.

"Ooooohh, there is another car coming! What do I do?"

"Try not to hit it," was my response, but that created even more panic, so I yelled at her to stop.

"How?" was her anxious response. By now the other car was almost a block away. "Brake ... brake!" I shouted, then next I turned the ignition off, and poor Irene was almost in tears. It was my fault, of course. Lesson one was a disaster, plain and simple.

Some years later, we again decided that Irene should drive. We were living in the country and had a long driveway and big yard, perfect for on-site training and practice. Irene was doing well and I prided myself on being a good driving instructor. How does that saying go again? Pride comes before a fall? One evening, we were going out and I asked if Irene would start the car and back it out of the garage, while I locked up and brought the kids to the car. As I approached the car, I could hear the engine running, and then revving-up while she was trying to back out. Fortunately she had the car in first gear, and drove it over the lawnmower, stalling against the garage wall. I say it was fortunate that she picked the wrong gear because if she had backed up, as intended, she would have run over me and the kids. All I had to do was jack the car up and remove what was left of the lawnmower. The howling soon died down, the tears stopped, and away we went. There were no more lessons, not until several years later with a real driving instructor.

Training is important, after all, when you want to change people's habits and thinking in some way, you must educate them into accepting your line of thinking. That is why you need teachers and career counsellors.

If it is a radical idea or ideology that you are trying to impart, then you start on the youth, like Adolf Hitler did (with such horrible effectiveness) with the Hitlerjugend. Indoctrinate them. You may not remember, but his little youth group was eventually counted at over a million strong and those poor impressionable teens were fighting ready.

Well that was back then. Today's sophisticated young people would never fall for that ... or would they?

It just so happens that our universities and colleges are hotbeds for liberal ideology-promoting "professors" (instructors), some even with criminal records and murder convictions in their pasts, and they seem to have the freedom to impose their ideas on students. Critical thinking must be taught, but in a balanced way. The presentations of the instructors must be delivered in a neutral fashion to allow proper critical thinking to take place.

Critical thinking ... critical thinking? Is that really necessary? Aren't you supposed to be taught all those different ideas that they talk about in college? Are you sure that you are in the right place?

Now what?

Is just plain thinking not good enough for someone like you?

Okay mom just leave it alone!

The Blaze reports:

EDUCATION
The stunning 355-page mega report that
reveals the radical curriculum at one American

college (and how a golf game gone awry led to it all)
Apr. 8, 2013 9:30pm Mytheos Holt

Bowdoin College, an elite university located in Maine, has recently found itself the nexus of a massive influx of controversy.

… And it's all because its president talked down the wrong person.

Bowdoin President Barry Mills reportedly engaged in a golf game during the summer of last year with philanthropist and investor Thomas Klingenstein who, while not being a graduate of Bowdoin, was himself interested in the college's approach to education. The result was an apparently awkward conversation during which Klingenstein complained of Bowdoin's excessive celebration of "racial and ethnic difference," in his words, rather than of "common American identity."

It is unclear precisely how sharp the conversation got, but it evidently distressed Mills enough that he decided to mention Klingenstein (albeit not by name) in his subsequent commencement address as a particularly unpleasant golfing partner who'd interrupted his backswing to spout racist platitudes.

Needless to say, Klingenstein found this response galling. What he decided to do about it, however, is almost certainly unprecedented: Klingenstein decided to commission researchers to do an academic report on Bowdoin's culture, both academically and outside the classroom, to see just what the college was teaching its students. The result was a 355-page report by the conservative National Association of Scholars that systematically broke down Bowdoin's entire culture and worldview with extreme frankness. The Blaze took a look at this report, and spoke to one of its authors, and you may be alarmed at the results.

What did that report find? That Bowdoin College, and indeed most of its peers in the elite liberal arts college community, is in fact:

A) Obsessed with identity politics to the point of using them as an excuse to teach irrelevant and/or trivial courses, and to admit under-qualified and under-educated students

B) At once entirely unconcerned with fostering healthy sexual behavior in students and consumed with making sure they follow inconsistent and ideologically motivated norms; and

C) Disingenuous in their purported support for critical thinking, which only extends as far

as thinking critically about topics which the
college finds institutionally inconvenient

The report, which runs 355 pages, is split into
two sections — first, there is the preface,
which assesses the facts regarding Bowdoin
and makes specific value judgments regarding
those facts. Second, there is the report itself,
which only explains the college's behavior
without passing judgment on it. The evidence
for each of the above conclusions is too ample
to rehearse in full, but a few highlights can
be offered as examples to illustrate just what
Bowdoin teaches. [14]

The report goes on showing Bowdoin in a **not** so flattering
way.

The United Nations has also found its way into our educational institutions, offering "opportunities" for students
to become involved in "Model UN Conferences", which are
appealing and have a lot to offer the student, including sur-
reptitious indoctrination. Teaching that globalization is here to
stay, and that it is good for everyone, the UN has the audacity
to indoctrinate our world's youth as if it were a legal, ruling,
world-authoritative governing body.

My friend attended several Model UN Conferences at our
local (and other) universities; she was impressed and quite

---

14   The Stunning 355-Page Mega Report That Reveals the Radical.., http://
     www.theblaze.com/stories/2013/04/08/the-stunning-355-page-mega-
     reportpthat-reveals-the-radical-curriculum-at-one-american-college-and-
     how-a-golf-game-gone-awry-led-to-it-all. (accessed Aug. 05 2013)

pleased with the whole thing. My granddaughter's husband was scheduled to take a group of his students from Kuwait to Moscow, Russia, for a Model UN Conference. It was cancelled at the last moment to his displeasure. The Middle East has a reputation for abruptly changing people's plans. Another of our granddaughters attended a Model UN Conference, but for her one conference was enough and she went back to more important things?

Education, starts the day we are born and is such an important part of the early stages of life that as such we should realise the importance of the mother and her role in the baby's life. We must realise that as our very early impressions of what is around us depends on our mothers and how they care for us, the security they provide becomes an important part of our lives. Later it should be a balanced experience in which the student learns truth and discernment, taught by honest and dedicated, trained instructors following an approved curriculum.

Let's start with basic education.

7. Prayer in schools

They used to start the day with student prayer in most public schools both in America and Canada. This is no longer allowed in our countries, yet we talk about freedom of speech and freedom of religion. No problem with sex education and other items of the curriculum that do not enhance education such as Yoga, derived from the Hindi and Buddhist religions.

So they teach them about sex, which seems to find little objection and suggest great activities?

Meanwhile back at the ranch in Canada there is another storm brewing, which has to do with kids from Muslim families attending public schools in Ontario. Attending public schools is a privilege, and the schools are financed through public means: taxes—the money that is collected from people who work for a living. School boards are the regulatory bodies that run the schools, and enforce the curriculum and standards for behaviour in those schools. If a parent or a student does not agree with the school or school board's rules, they are well advised to seek enrolment in a private school that has rules more to their liking.

For many years now, prayer in public schools has not been practised, not because of the prolonged fight to keep prayer in the schools, but because of the Anti-Christian movement that has been afoot since Madalyn Murray O'Haire won her victory as an American atheist. Many discussions and meetings later, that situation has not really changed. There are many people actively trying to keep it that way. For Muslims to expect that the rules should be changed to suit *them* goes contrary to reason. …. Oh really?

The Toronto Star reports:

> Protesters oppose Muslim prayer in public schools
> Muslim prayers at a Toronto middle school prompt protest at the board office.
> By: Tess Kalinowski Staff Reporter
> Published on Mon Jul 25 2011
>
> They waved signs that warned of "creeping jihad" and proclaimed "Islam must be reformed or banned." They chanted —"No Islam in our schools"; "No Mohamed in our schools"; "No Sharia law in our country."
>
> About 100 protesters, many from groups such as the Jewish Defense League, the Christian Heritage Party and Canadian Hindu Advocacy, came to the Toronto District School Board Monday evening to protest its approval of formal Friday prayer services for Muslim students at Valley Park Middle School.
>
> Standing at the back of the crowds, far from the megaphone-wielding speakers, York University students Mariam Hamaoui and Sarah Zubaira had their own signs espousing their right to

pray in school. They came to thank the school board for providing a place for the Valley Park students to pray. Previously those students had left their school to attend prayers at a nearby mosque on Fridays.

Bringing an imam into the school was a means of preventing some of the approximately 300 Muslim students from failing to return to classes after those prayers, said school board director Chris Spence. It also meant they don't have to cross a busy street.

Valley Park has been holding the prayers in the cafeteria for three years and there have been no complaints within the school community of about 1,200, he said.

Hamaoui, 18, said she had to go to the basement to pray when she attended Etobicoke Collegiate Institute because "there was no other place."

"I think people should be open minded. I don't see the problem to go pray. Praying is helping everybody," she told reporters and the protesters who aggressively confronted her.

"Universities let anybody pray. I don't see the problem with having middle schools," she told one woman. To a man who told her that prayer belonged at home, she said, "Is our school not a second home?"

"It's our constitutional right," said Zubaira, who wore a hijab for the first time on Monday. Speaking to reporters inside the school board office, Spence said schools have an obligation to religious accommodation. "It's not a matter of if we should be doing it — it's how," he said. But, "accommodation is fluid. It's not written in stone," said Spence, who added the board is feeling its way on the difficult issue.

Outside on the board steps, Toronto grandmother Frances Flynt said she came to the protest to "oppose having a mosque in a school." She said her grandchildren are only permitted to sing secular songs like Jingle Bells at Christmas. "They're not allowed to sing hymns in school," she said.

Artist and atheist Ryan Browne came alone to the protest. "I felt so strongly about it I decided I'd come down and do something about it," he said, adding that he fears "our public institutions can be apprehended by certain interest groups."

(When I read this, I wondered if the Muslim kids are exempted from sex education or if they are to be exposed to that—after all this is a taboo subject for Muslims.) (Author)

"I work for the TDSB (Toronto District School Board), I try to teach in an environment of equity. I just find this kind of rhetoric intolerant," said Omar Qayum, a Muslim math teacher at Agincourt Collegiate. For the past five years, he says, he's been taking time on Fridays to pray with his students and there have been no problems.

"We have a Catholic school system. It is publicly funded. My tax dollars go to Catholic schools. I don't have a problem so long as other religious groups have that same right, but that's not the case . . . When they talk about gender segregation, we have Catholic schools that are all girls and all boys. It's just that Muslims are easy targets. We are a minority. Islamophobia is an industry these days," said Qayum. [15]

Tess Kalinowski, *Toronto Star*

Really Mr. Qayum? The school is property of the province and the Toronto School District operates it as a public school, as you should know, you work for the school board don't you?

With all the schools being busy trying to educate students, how can they find the time to deal with the many complaints about the Muslim kids' demands for special treatment? Again

---

15 Protesters oppose Muslim prayer in public schools | Toronto Star, http://www.thestar.com/life/parent/2011/07/25/protesters_oppose_muslim_prayer_in_public_schools/html (accesssed Sept. 20 2012)

we go back to London, Ontario. Wow those Londoners are trouble makers. Must be Canadians, eh?

Next we find another school caves:

Toronto Sun reports:

> Muslim prayer room opens in Catholic high
> school 369
> DALE CARRUTHERS, QMI AGENCY
> FIRST POSTED: MONDAY, SEPTEMBER 17,
> 2012 01:34 PM EDT | UPDATED: MONDAY,
> SEPTEMBER 17, 2012 02:03 PM EDT
>
> LONDON, ONT. — Mother Teresa Catholic secondary school is turning a second-floor office into an Islamic prayer room — the first high school in the city, private or public, to do so. Carpet will soon cover the tile flooring, speakers will be installed and prayer mats purchased to provide the school's Muslim students, estimated at around two dozen, with a quiet and private place to pray.
>
> The idea has been in the works since the end of the last school year after a group of Muslim students lobbied administration to create the space. "They're members of our school community. We want to ensure that all our students feel welcome, that they feel that they belong," said Principal Ana Paula Fernandes. The prayer room, expected to be completed by the end of September, is located on a busy stretch on the

second floor, just metres from the school's large chapel. "That was very important to ensure that it was included in the main building, and not tucked away somewhere," Fernandes said.

Grade 12 student Amir Farhi, 17, was part of the group that led the push for the prayer room. "We do have quite a bit of Muslims in this school who find it hard to practice their religion," he said. "Having this prayer room, it's easy for them to do their Friday prayers."

Though Muslims pray facing Mecca, Saudi Arabia, five times a day, the room will mainly be used Fridays, the holiest day of the week in Islam. Administration and students are working with a local imam, a leader of Islamic worship services, to create guidelines governing use of the room. "We just want to come together as a community, exchange our beliefs, sharing our ideas and helping grow this school with its values," said Farhi, who applauded school officials for moving so quickly to create the room.

While baptism is a requirement to attend Catholic elementary schools, students of any faith can enrol at Catholic secondary schools. No figure is available on how many of Mother Teresa's 1,400 students are non-Catholic, but

Fernandes said the school's diverse population is one of its strengths.

The prayer room will also foster tolerance and understanding of different religions among non-Muslim students, Fernandes added. "It certainly is meant to strengthen the sense of community and the sense of respect . . . for one's peers and the community at large."[16]

dale.carruthers@sunmedia.ca

It is not the Muslims wanting to have prayer that bothers me but rather the fact that Muslim's demands are given in to, while prayer in public schools by all other religions has been banned. Are the Muslims also attending Catholic schools to get around the prayer ban in public schools? What is next?

I read that article and I think "Pardon me, but am I hearing this right? Around two dozen Muslim kids are finding it hard to practice their religion in a Catholic school? Hmm ... would it be easier for Catholic or Protestant kids to practice their religion in a Muslim school? Only in Canada!

I wonder if they have prayer rooms for kids of other faiths, or if the approximately 24 Muslim kids present such a force that even Catholic schools fear reprisal if the Muslim demands are not accommodated?

An amazing change in our school systems has occurred over the years since prayer and discipline were removed from the

---

16 Muslim prayer room opens in Catholic high school | Ontario .., http://www.torontosun.com/2012/09/17/muslim-prayer-room-opens-in-catholic-high-school (accessed Sept.20 2012)

classrooms. Schools are becoming more and more unpleasant, as there appears to be very little respect for either the teachers or the students.

Let me step back here for a moment. When I say that schools are becoming more and more unpleasant, I wasn't talking about those cases where teachers and students have become emotionally involved and had sexual affairs.

The increased security measures that have to be taken, requiring the installation of metal detectors and now even armed, security personnel in some schools and colleges, is shocking. Bullying is increasing with the result that some kids actually commit suicide. Bullying is making the social media even less social than it was before.

North America has a great love for sports and college sports' teams are extremely popular with a large part of the population. The national sports' leagues are big business and fans go to great lengths to support their teams, even travelling great distances to take in a game played by "their team." When I see the enthusiasm displayed when people talk about a game they have watched, they remember so much detail and have praise for their heroes, I envy them.

Whichever sport it may be, hockey, baseball or football, I just can never get too excited about it. That's me! I'm not into yelling and screaming about anything in my life but that does not mean I can't enjoy myself. What thrills me is when I see the coach or captain of a team stop to pray with the team before a game, what a great example these guys are to their fans and audience, TV or otherwise.

Oh my goodness, education is a touchy subject—one of our own making. My feeling is that there should be a simple rule that applies to all schools countrywide. Have a standard approved curriculum for all grades up to grade twelve, to be used by public and private schools alike. Restore respect and order in the classroom through discipline, enacted by the teacher and assisted by another school staff member.

The lack of respect for authority and each other is a basic flaw in our society, emulated by teen idols like Justin Bieber and Miley Cirus. Also, there are many others who have found fame and fortune, but live as horrible examples to our youth.

In private schools, there should be time for prayer and religious teaching aside from the regular standard curriculum. Colleges/Universities should also adhere to teaching an approved curriculum, and use the applicable disciplines of technology or academia.

All school or college staff should have to pass a rigorous background check, aside from the academic qualifications for the position, in order to qualify.

When I see the professional sports' teams pray before a game,
I say let's bring back prayer in all our schools.

8. Our Freedom in jeopardy?

While we are busy keeping our daily lives in order, and working hard, we must also have our time off for relaxation. Most of us have hobbies or play sports that we find relaxing and enjoy, I love to sail my boat as much as I can, which never seems to be enough! It wasn't always like that.

Remember when we would be entitled to two weeks of paid vacation after a full year of work, and after eight or ten years we might be allowed three weeks? Today, many jobs begin with three weeks vacation, and I know of some that, after several years of service, have as much as nine weeks of paid vacation time per year. The term "flexible time" is used often to describe a workweek that changes the operating hours to suit the individual. These give a greater freedom to the individual worker, allowing them to spend more time relaxing with friends, and doing favourite things.

Often have I been jealous of schoolteachers, having six or eight weeks of summer vacation time. I could take that sailing trip I just never had enough time for, or paint the house all in one summer and still have enough time left over for a nice camping trip!

Now my feelings are of concern for the teachers. The violence in schools has increased in frequency in recent years, and in severity as well, with mass-murder shootings on the increase. So many lives—children, teachers, other adults— senselessly destroyed. It affects families, friends, and even whole communities.

Each time such a horrendous crime takes place, the gun control debate goes into full swing, but the real problem never seems to be addressed properly. The real problem must be with the person doing the shooting. Often there are lame excuses as reasons why the individual lost his/her mind and goes on a rampage.

One of the most controversial subjects is gun control, and of course there are many others that come into play as well, when we start something we haven't done for a while or something altogether new. Gun control, however, is a very important subject that brings out the best and the worst in people, and there are no simple answers—considering that in countries with some form of restrictive or total gun control the crime rate is not any less. Let me stress that not all crime is gun-related. In areas where permits are issued to legally carry concealed weapons, the crime rates have dropped to some extent.

The US second amendment was created for the reason of keeping citizens' safe. The second amendment must be pro-tected 'as is' because if allowed to be changed or taken from the constitution, by those with a poorly thought-out agenda, it will be gone forever.

There are several versions of the text of the Second Amendment, each with slight capitalization and punctuation differences, found in the official documents surrounding the adoption of the Bill of Rights.

The ***Bill of Rights*** *as passed by the Congress:*

> *A well regulated Militia, being necessary to the*
> *security of a free State, the right of the people*
> *to keep and bear Arms, shall not be infringed.* [17]

Gun control is not altogether bad, but in many cases it has proven to be ineffective in reducing crime. The big problem with gun control is that the proponents tend to propose ridiculous laws that target the lawful gun owner, not the criminal. There are many aspects of gun ownership that require responsibility and a serious, rigid training program should be one of the requirements before ownership be granted. Any gun control laws, to be effective, must be enforced by an authority such as a police force or similar law enforcement agency.

Some games like laser tag and paintball tend to muddy the waters, as young children and adolescents come away from these games often with the illusion that they used real guns.

They looked realistic and so they killed only to have their victims get up and come along to go for a burger with them afterwards. This, I believe, clouds their understanding of reality and makes it difficult to know what is real and what isn't. Arcade and video games that some youngsters play for hours on end are also conditioning their minds to unrealistic expectations of their actions. Some of these games are so awful and brutal that it makes me shudder.

---

17 Talk:United States Bill of Rights — Wikisource, the free .., http://
en.wikisource.org/wiki/Talk:United_STates_Bill_of_Rights (accessed May
18 2013)

In addition to the games, we have a movie industry that takes delight in using gun power to tell a story of fiction; the movie industry is very skilled in making a situation look realistic. To see the star of the movie gun down several people without any show of emotion. It blurs the lines of what is real and what is not.

Years ago my wife's stepfather, Harry, had his house broken into; the unfortunate burglar didn't count on anyone being home. The would-be burglar was surprised by eighty year-old Harry, who armed and in his pyjamas, chased him out of the house. Shuffling along while emptying his pistol, but only once hitting his target, apparently he wounded the burglar in his leg. The guy got away and never came back. The house now was decorated with five bullet holes, making a good conversation point.

Some time later we were visiting my in-laws and the children were playing around when one of them, about five years old, came wandering into the living room carrying a nice loaded pistol which he found under Harry's bed.

No harm was done but it could have been so different. Harry learned an important lesson that day, not to leave anything like a loaded gun lying around where anyone could take it. The rule after that incident became, "no loaded guns anywhere and always trigger locked, separate from the ammunition and locked away."

Canadian gun laws are quite good now and require a person to take a course in gun safety before applying for a permit to purchase and own a gun. This permit is subject to a background check by the RCMP and when qualified, the prospective gun owner needs to be a member in good standing of a sport shooting club, rod and gun club, or similar association, before making a legal purchase. The next step is critical as the RCMP will then register the gun by fully printing the gun barrel's internal markings, make, model and numbers for the registration, along with the owner's personal particulars. Next they assign the shortest route between the owner's home and his shooting club, as the allowed route of transport for the gun. Only then are you allowed to have your own gun and take it home, via the shortest route between the police station and your home, of course. This applies to legal handguns and their owners only.

Criminal and illegal ownership presents a whole different problem and is impossible to deal with outside the courts.

Remember, last year when a military man in England had his head chopped off with a big knife, a machete, the police could not respond as there were no firearms in the nearest precinct and they were not willing to risk their own necks, literally; crime cannot be legislated away. I wonder how Piers Morgan would react to that situation?

If, with a magic wand all firearms could be swept away, there would no longer be any gun-related crimes. Magic belongs in fairy tales and children's stories but in real life gun control remains a very difficult problem. The Canadian government seems to have a good, but not perfect system. The background check is a very important part of reducing firearms-related crimes. In the United States, the detailed background check is often discussed as a procedure to enhance their gun acquisition procedure.

As mentioned earlier, gun control is not at all a simple issue. My heart breaks when I see the results of careless handling and storage of firearms, the victims so often being young children. We can't legislate crime away and we cannot make people act more responsibly, but a good start would be training every prospective gun owner in the responsible handling and use of guns.

Most responsible gun owners have their handguns primarily for sport target shooting and long guns for hunting.

This next article appeared on "The Blaze TV."

As reported on The Blaze TV
Shocking proposed law would give sheriff
access to the
homes of gun owners
Tuesday, Feb 19, 2013 at 1:13 PM PST
The Blaze TV

In California they are confiscating tens of thousands of legally purchased firearms while in Washington State a new law has been proposed that would allow the sheriff to inspect the home of an assault weapon owner one time per year. How far will gun regulations go?

"Well, Senate Bill 5737 out of Olympia, Washington would ban the sale of semi-automatic weapons that use detachable magazines," Glenn said on radio this morning. "it would ban the use of a semiautomatic that uses the detachable magazine and magazines that contain more than 10 rounds. But here's the -- here's the best part of it: In order to continue to possess an assault weapon that was legally possessed on the effective date of this section, the person possessing shall safely and securely store the assault weapon and the sheriff of the county may, may, but no more than once per year, conduct an inspection of the house," Glenn said.

"I'm pretty sure that I'm not having the sheriff come over to my house," Glenn said. "To inspect my guns and my house and to search to make sure I don't have any other illegal weapons. I don't think I'm for that. "

"Lance Palmer, Seattle trial lawyer says to the Seattle Times, they always say we'll never go house to house to get your guns, but when you see this, you have to wonder."

The Seattle Times spoke with two democrats who admitted the bill shows why conservatives worry about encroaching government and that the provisions in the bill needed to be eliminated: Responding to the Newtown school massacre, the bill would ban the sale of semi-automatic weapons that use detachable ammunition magazines. Clips that contain more than 10 rounds would be illegal.

But then, with respect to the thousands of weapons like that already owned by Washington residents, the bill says this: "In order to continue to possess an assault weapon that was legally possessed on the effective date of this section, the person possessing shall ... safely and securely store the assault weapon. The sheriff of the county may, no more than once per year, conduct an inspection to ensure compliance with this subsection."

In other words, come into homes without a warrant to poke around. Failure to comply could get you up to a year in jail.

"I'm a liberal Democrat — I've voted for only one Republican in my life," Palmer told me. "But now I understand why my right-wing opponents worry about having to fight a government takeover." He added: "It's exactly this sort of thing that drives people into the arms of the NRA [National Rifle Association]."

I have been blasting the NRA for its paranoia in the gun-control debate. But Palmer is right — you can't fully blame them, when cops going door-to-door show up in legislation.

I spoke to two of the sponsors. One, Sen. Adam Kline, D-Seattle, a lawyer who typically is hyper-attuned to civil-liberties issues, said he did not know the bill authorized police searches because he had not read it closely before signing on.

"I made a mistake," Kline said. "I frankly should have vetted this more closely."

That lawmakers sponsor bills they haven't read is common, not good but common. Still, it's disappointing on one of this political magnitude. Not counting a long table, it's only an eight-page bill.

"That tells you a lot too about just about every bill that's been passed in the past four years because nobody reads them. They don't know what's in them," Pat said.

"We have a bill in Missouri where they're saying basically the same things, that you're going to get rid of all of them and if you're caught with them, it becomes a felony. Now you have it in Washington State. I mean, have you tried to buy bullets lately?" Glenn said.

Glenn explained that gun prices were rising and in many places it was hard to find guns in stock. Bullets and primers that are used to make ammunition are also difficult to purchase in stores due to short supplies. [18]

The Blaze TV

---

[18] Shocking proposed law would give sheriff access to the homes .., http://www.glennbeck.com/2013/02/19/shocking-porposed-law-would-give-sheriff-access-to-the-homes-of-gun-owners/ (accessed Feb. 20 2013)

When a government agency becomes involved in a covert operation, it is usually intended to catch and correct some wrongdoing. The US operation, "Fast and Furious", was designed to catch criminals in the illegal drug trade. A number of firearms were sold to gunrunners who supply the drug cartels with firearms. Fast and Furious originated with officials at the Bureau of Alcohol, Tobacco and Firearms. Tracking the guns became difficult and the Mexican officials were upset with the influx of illegal weapons.

Those weapons were sold to known gunrunners, criminals who only deal with other criminals; no wonder the Mexican officials were upset.

It was a dismal failure of an outrageous plan by government officials! You're not playing with toys but real guns fellas and so far your failed plan has cost a number of lives, both Mexican and American lives!

Don't you find it confusing when a government that seems so determined on taking guns from its citizens sells thousands of guns into the hands of illegal drug traffickers and the drug cartel elite? Then, when caught, the government officials lie, lie, and lie some more about it. Do they get in trouble over it? Not too likely with Barack Obama in the driver's seat. It's just like the Benghazi, Libya debacle. Four Americans lose their lives and nobody is held accountable, yet we know that there were advance warnings of danger, and that the people involved (like Hillary Clinton) did nothing to help the situation, and the same goes for Barack Obama. They lie about the reasons for the attack, refuse to answer questions about their actions (or lack thereof) and go free.

To work or not to work that is a serious question

Freedom to work has become very limited, because the unions exercise strong control in many industries and organizations. Entering into some work situations requires a membership in a union and others require you to join a union as soon as you get the job. However, in both cases there is no choice of opting out of membership if you want the job. Next comes paying the union dues, which are often used for political activities, such as making donations to help elect certain politicians—mostly without the approval of the membership, often reasons for disputes at the union meetings. As a matter of public record, a lot of union money (millions of dollars of membership dues) went to pay for putting Barack Obama in the White House.

If you're a conservative, you may well ask yourself, where is the freedom of choice in this?

We can all have our personal choices as long as it is the same as theirs.

Henry Ford once said:

"Any customer can have a car painted any color that he wants so long as it is Black."

The few non-union jobs are often just as well paying, with the same benefits as the union jobs that are often not considered "performance important" enough to relate to salary. It is difficult for me to understand that. Within a group of ten employees, there will be some good workers and some mediocre workers, but three (for example) are exceptional. In a union shop, they all would get the same pay.

But if the shop is not a union shop, and the employees can be paid according to their performance, then there will be an incentive for all to do their best.

For some, the question (to work or not to work) is quickly answered. They know that they are better off not working, since welfare pays them more than minimum wages once medical, dental and other benefits are considered! This attitude creates an entitlement problem. One of the underlying reasons for this is a problem with society: the breakdown of the family unit, which has far-reaching effects. Another reason is the widespread drug use in our society today, which brings with it an inability to work and varying degrees of criminal behaviour, from petty theft to murder.

The drug cartels are a murderous bunch who will stop at nothing to conduct their business, and the cost of human lives is too high to be ignored by even the least-interested governments. But even at the local level, drug addiction has a way of taking lives. Slowly or fast, it so often kills.

Holland, or the Netherlands, whatever you want to call it, has the dubious reputation of being very liberal about drug use and Amsterdam seems to have become a haven for the drug culture. This liberal attitude has had a serious result on the many non-users because of the crime associated with the drug addicts' way of life. My sister and brother-in-law lived in one of the nicest homes, located in an idyllic setting at the edge of a park in my hometown. They lived there for many years, but had to sell their home and move away because of the serious crime situation. After several break-ins, they could not go out at night unless one stayed behind.

The cavalier attitude about drug use and the legalization thereof has worn off; many liberal people in Holland have changed their minds about it, however now it is difficult to reverse.

A wise, old Russian once said:

"The United States will not fall in war, but to the enslavement of drug addiction."

He may have had a point. The war against the drug cartels is not a war that the government is likely to win any time soon. The greed of dirty money fuels the widespread addiction problems, and seems to be gaining ground.

There are few people who have not been touched by drug abuse somewhere within their circle of friends and/or family. Most of us know some horror stories of those involved in drug abuse and the painful family situations they have had to endure. So far, the medical profession has not been able to come up with a cure for addiction problems that is effective, but there are some medications that are an alternative to the illegal drug use. Similarly, the abuse of alcohol is still a problem that has not been solved in our society.

Becoming addicted or enslaved means becoming dependent. This simply means that, in yet another area of life, we lose our independence or freedom.

There. Apathy again. Someone says, "Apathy kills", and another one asks, "Who cares?"

Well now we are losing some things because of changing rules, regulations, substance abuse, and of course, entitlement.

New regulations are coming from all three levels of government—federal, state/provincial, and municipal—some influenced by the United Nations. As the regulations are put into place, we see that some are needed and good, but not all of them fall into that category.

The world as we know it today is full of strife and conflicts. "Wars and rumours of wars"[19] are on the news daily. Prevention of this was attempted many years ago, through the creation of the United Nations, in an attempt to facilitate peace among its member nations. Although successful at first, this seems to have failed.

The UN Agenda 21 doesn't hide the fact that the UN has an overall plan that could eventually affect literally everyone. The plan stresses the need for worldwide control of resources, and the consumption thereof, in order to wipe out poor health, poverty, and hunger in the world, a novel and noble idea but definitely wide open to misuse and abuse.

The function and mandate of the UN organization seems to have changed. Membership has been granted to nations once deemed to be the enemy, and the original rules and regulations have lost out to new ideas.

Now we have branches of the UN interfering with agriculture, as well as other things, like federal elections, in the countries that are already running smoothly with their own agencies in control of those areas. This is creating frustration for many who believe that we are losing control to an organization that was originally created to avoid this kind of dictatorship.

Remember?

---

19 Mathew 24:6

The <u>Principles</u> of the United Nations:

- All Member States have sovereign equality.

- All Member States must obey the Charter.

- Countries must try to settle their differences by peaceful means.

- Countries must avoid using force or threatening to use force.

- **The UN may not interfere in the domestic affairs of any country.**

- Countries should try to assist the United Nations.

I am slowly beginning to feel the boa constrictor effect on our freedom, which is being taken away a little bit at a time. The slow squeeze doesn't hurt at first, but after a while it becomes painful and restrictive. Am I alone out here or do you have similar feelings? Is there enough evidence of what I see, hear, and feel to make you concerned also? Are we on the brink of a breakdown or is there still some sanity out there?

There is a lot of talk making reference to a global community, a global village, and some heating system called global warming. I must admit that I haven't been able to find the global village, but it seems to me that in time the global community and global village are going to try and have a global government. maybe globally it will be called The New World Order?

It keeps coming back to this very same thing!
Stick to the principles; even the United Nations

must not interfere in the domestic affairs of a member country.

As I mentioned earlier, the world as we know it today is full of strife and conflicts , with wars and rumours of wars on the news every day. Instead of trying to prevent this, the UN is shaping up to take over in many areas, the world's political arena, world health care, world economics, education, and the redistribution of the world's wealth.

Meanwhile North Korea is playing a very dangerous game, threatening to start a nuclear war, and we could be stuck in the middle of it. North Korea's leader, Kim Jong-un has youth on his side. This young ruler appears to be fearless and full of ... um ... what do you call it ... oh yeah, energy. This guy is a real sweetheart. He recently had his Uncle, Jang Song-Thaek executed on trumped-up charges. Just what the world needs now, a trigger-happy, fearless youngster with some atomic toys, taunting other leaders with his rhetoric and the power to back up his threats.

Ahhh .... I want my mommy!

Well my mother was strong through both World Wars, but she isn't much help in this situation. My father and mother had their share of war misery, and I'm glad they are no longer burdened with today's wars and rumours of wars.

Let's hope that we don't get drawn into more wars (peace-keeping) by being connected to the UN since there are members of the UN that were considered hostile nations before they got membership in the organization.

Does a nation lose its hostility toward other nations after becoming a member of the United Nations?

As mentioned before some of the countries now members of the United Nations were, to put it mildly, HOSTILE Nations to the United States and other members of the United Nations' organization.

During President Jimmy Carter's days, the Iranian relationship with the US deteriorated rapidly. In January 1979, the chaotic state of affairs in the country was reason for Secretary of State, Cyrus Vance, to order the evacuation from Iran of all American nationals, government employees and non-government contractors and their families. The only remaining Americans were the essential government employees; approximately 45 000 Americans fled from Iran.

On February 14, 1979, the US Embassy in Tehran was invaded. The marines held off the invaders until the Ambassador gave the order to stand down and moved the staff to the upstairs of the building while the marines flooded the lower part of the building with tear gas. Ambassador Sullivan appealed to Khomeini and some time later Khomeini placed a group of men outside the Embassy for protection.

On the same day, the US Ambassador to Afghanistan, Adolph Dubs, was kidnapped and murdered in Kabul.

On November 4, 1979, the embassy was attacked again and this time the defense was made up of 13 US marines and a few Iranian police. It was over quickly and all Americans in the building were captured. I remember seeing them bound and blind-folded, being paraded outside before the television cameras as an Iranian victory. Fifty two hostages were taken and six officials eluded capture. They hid in the Canadian and Swedish embassies. The leader nicknamed "Ayatollah Dollar," was in charge all during the occupation. Among the Iranians that were identified at the time was Hamid Aboutalebi.

The six officials hiding in the Canadian and Swedish Embassies were smuggled out of Iran using Canadian passports. The Iranians that were involved with the incident in the Tehran Embassy kept the 52 Americans hostage for 444 days. The hostages were released in January of 1981, shortly after President Ronald Reagan took office.

Hostage taking is an act of terrorism and a serious crime, invading an Embassy of any country is also a serious crime and usually ends with serious results or consequences. In this case the US and Iranian relations were, to say the least, 'soured' and not easily forgotten or restored.

Today, some 33 years later, the American Government and thus the American people are asked to forgive and forget the hostage taking in Tehran by granting Mr. Hamid Aboutalebi a visa to the US, all because the Iranian government saw fit to appoint Mr. Hamid Aboutalebi as an Ambassador to the UN. This is obviously an act of defiance to the US and is meant to further aggravate any relationship that remains between the two countries.

Mr. UN Ambassador Hamid Aboutalebi has already actively served his country in Belgium and Italy. It shows a further weakening of the US political power in the world today and is almost directly linked to the Obama administration, which is not awe inspiring at all. Mr. Mahmoud Ahmadinejad, the Iranian President from August 2009, to August, 2013, was determined to have nuclear arms in his arsenal and accomplished much of his goals. In August, 2013, President Mahmoud Ahmadinejad lost the election and was replaced by the more moderate President, Hassan Rouhani. Now, if this President Hassan Rouhani, is a moderate, why appoint Mr. Hamid Aboutalebi as an ambassador to the UN, especially considering his past involvement with terrorism against the US. This also shows contempt for the US by the UN in accepting the appointment!

Ahhh.... Now I really want my mommy!

We have fought wars for the freedom of others,
Let's not lose our OWN freedom due to apathy!

9. The Korean, Vietnam and other wars

The Korean peninsula was home to all Koreans until 1945 when the country was divided into North and South Korea; the dividing line or border was drawn along the 38th parallel. Tensions and border incidents cost many lives and there seemed no solution to stop these incidents of provocation.

Tensions remained between the two countries until 1950 when North Korea invaded South Korea with about 75,000 troops, apparently supported by Russia.

After some time of monitoring the conflict in Korea, the USA came to the aid of South Korea. President Harry Truman was all for defending South Korea to avoid Russia getting a strong foothold in that part of the world. The military, with General Douglas MacArthur in command, came to defend South Korea and start peace negotiations. The war lasted till 1953, and the peace negotiations also came to an end. Total peace was never accomplished; tensions and incidents at the border are still ongoing.

The war cost approximately 40,000 American and 100,000+ Korean lives. It is hard to believe those high sacrifices were made by so many people without a clear victory.

During the Cold War years, Vietnam, Laos and Cambodia, were at odds with each other and Communism repeatedly was blamed for disruptions and conflicts in the area. The

Vietcong, a Communist group in South Vietnam became active in terrorism and guerilla warfare, and dissention caused many to sympathize with them.

Ho Chi Minh, president of North Vietnam took credit for expelling the French from Vietnam (French Indochina) and intended to reunify North and South Vietnam and with the help of the Vietcong, it would become one Communist state.

The United States of America got involved in order to stop the spreading of Communism, or at least contain it. The war raged from 1955 to 1973 when it was declared over. By 1975 North and South Vietnam were again one small Country.

The War cost 58,220 US lives and in excess of 1.3 million Vietnamese, Cambodian and Laotian lives were lost. This was another war without a clear victory and high loss of lives.

The Vietnam War is the most commonly used name for the Vietnam Conflict—involving on one side, the army of the Republic of Vietnam and the US Military, and on the other side, the North Vietnamese Army and the Viet Cong, a South-Vietnamese communist guerrilla force.

The Vietnam War has been referred to as "the war that could not be won."

Why is it that so many of the Vietnam vets have had such a difficult time re-entering civilian life upon returning state-side and home. It seems that never before have so many vets been plagued, after any of the previous wars, by those hard to deal with problems such as depression, post-traumatic stress-disorder, battle fatigue and other related issues.

What will be the future of the Iraq war, Libyan conflict vets and Afghanistan war vets; these wars have had NATO Nations involved. There will be many soldiers going home to their respective countries, will they be looked after, will there be an understanding of what they may be faced with? Will the numbers of homeless, hopeless vets increase over the next months and years? Or will there be some responsibility for having sent them into those difficult situations? Government excuses like shrinking budgets don't cut it with me, they took the initiative to send our men and women to do a job and risk their lives.

Look after them!

In the recent wars the casualties have shown results of extremely vicious ways used by the enemy to disable soldiers with roadside bomb attacks and grenades, heavier artillery amongst other things. Disabled vets often are so badly maimed for life that their families have difficulties adjusting to the needed changes in their homes and daily routines. When we know someone like that we can only reach out and extend a hand of help and love.

Those Vietnam vets that survived and are still alive, who went to war to keep the communists at bay, are still losing. The pain and suffering that I have seen in some of my friends ... they will never recover from "Nam". And those who have taken their own lives because of the haunting memories ... oh Lord. Heaven help us all.

War is HELL!

Now we know that war is an activity, or exercise, in which we expect one side to win and the other side to lose. However, it doesn't always work out that way. Wars have been fought in which there could not be a winner declared. Take the Iraq war for instance. It started because of suspicion that there were weapons of mass destruction in Iraq, just waiting to be used. Official reports were confusing and inaccurate. Not too surprisingly the existence of the weapons of mass destruction, was denied by Iraq's president at the time, Saddam Hussein.

But who would believe Saddam Hussein after what he had done to his own people in Iraq. In 1988 he used chemical weapons against his own people in Halabja, Iraq, killing more than 7,000 people and causing a lot of after-effects for the survivors of the attack.

The United States and Britain were concerned that these weapons posed a threat to them and their allies. This triggered the Iraq war, but there was more to it than just the concern about weapons of mass destruction. They also wanted to bring Saddam Hussein to justice, and to establish a democracy in Iraq. This became a very controversial and painful war. It took many lives on both sides, with many wounded and maimed for life, and much devastation. Still, the alternatives may have been catastrophic.

There are people who have been involved with humanitarian work in Iraq before and since the pull out of the American military, and the situation has become more dangerous for Muslim and Christians alike. The work is very difficult, because the internal strife and conflicts have not stopped. Sunni and Shiite insurgents are continuing to fight and create trouble in Iraq. Persecution of Christians is in full swing. The Christian Church in Iraq is suffering much, and many Christians have left Iraq for more religious-tolerant countries.

But there are those who are not leaving, like Canon Andrew White—the "Vicar of Baghdad"—who, as the shepherd of the infidel minority Christians, is there because "God placed him there".

Recently, I watched Andrew White, nicknamed the "Vicar of Baghdad" being interviewed on CBC's "Context" with Lorna Dueck. I was struck with his compassion as he spoke about his calling as a minister and the losses that he has seen in his congregation—with more than a thousand killed in the last ten years. Many others have left for safer regions, yet the Vicar of Baghdad remains true to his calling in Iraq, and serves his church and congregation, even while suffering from multiple sclerosis, which has an affect on his speech as well as his mobility. If your life includes prayer, remember this man of God in your prayers. And if you do not usually pray, please start by praying for the Vicar of Baghdad, and the many persecuted Christians.

Although different in many ways from Pastor Richard Wurmbrand, whom I mentioned earlier, I noticed a definite similarity in their assessments of the North American Christians, and their feelings about our apathy regarding the persecuted Christians.

Pastor Richard Wurmbrand was jailed and tortured by the communists in Romania, whereas Canon Andrew White is in Iraq, which aside from being a Muslim country that is hostile toward Christians, is also still pretty much a war zone.

The September 11, 2001 terrorist attacks on America brought on another war, the hunt for terrorist leader Osama bin Laden, which started the war on terrorism. This war was difficult to fight because of the very nature of the enemy whose identity was not really known. It did evolve to some extent into the war in Afghanistan where a civil war had been ongoing for almost a decade. When the US asked the Taliban to give up Osama bin Laden they refused, then Great Britain and the United States of America joined forces to fight terrorism, the Taliban and al-Qaeda. Next NATO got involved and the allied forces have continued the fight on terrorism for well over a decade.

Since September 11, 2001 it would seem that many more Muslim women in North America have been easily identified by wearing clothing that is customary in Muslim countries. By doing so, they have made a statement about their faith that is commendable, but why have they only done so since September 11, 2001? Why not before that date? Is it because that terrible day is seen by some in the Muslim world as a day of coming out, as a victory in the quest to conquer the world for Allah? For Islam? I wonder.

Keeping the communists at bay in Korea was a relative success, but communism is not likely to be stopped by war, and since the Korean war, communism has been growing slowly in countries all around the world. The Muslim world is growing faster, and by infiltration, is readying its terrorist efforts all over the world. Yes, I know there are peace-loving Muslims, but the Koran teaches them to fight and destroy the "Infidel"—the non-Muslim. Let's be careful not to lose our freedom of religion, and our freedom of speech. Already there is a strong movement to take all our freedom away.

War is hell.

That is the conclusion I have come to. The human race is slow in learning that simple fact because there have been wars since time immemorial.

When Reality Hits

Isn't it time we learned to avoid war altogether?

10. Under Attack

Have you ever been under attack verbally? Have you been in a fistfight ... or been shot at and have the burning hot metal tear into your flesh? Just speak your mind about your ideals, and be passionate about it, and the attacks will follow—hopefully just verbal attacks. Even road rage can turn into physical attacks. An attack in military fashion is far more serious and involves combat, often with horrible results. Just think of some of the recent wars and the victims of modern warfare.

When a country is under attack, the attackers come in different shapes and forms and sometimes from within the country itself. In the past, presidents have been assassinated, which caused great sorrow and disruption in America. Those attacks were mostly politically motivated and created great concern in the country. In November of 1963, President J.F. Kennedy was assassinated, his accused assassin was murdered only a few days later while in custody, by Jack Ruby before a court appearance could take place. The country went into disbelief and shock as this beloved president was taken from us.

In 1968 R.F. Kennedy (Bobby) was a politician and had served as Attorney General under his brother President J.F. Kennedy and his successor, Lyndon, B. Johnson. While serving as senator for New York and campaigning for the presidency, he was assassinated by a 24 year-old Palestinian. This was another big loss for the Kennedy family and a big blow for American politics.

Also in 1968, amid racial unrest and strive, the well respected and beloved civil rights leader, Martin Luther King Jr. was assassinated, this created even more unrest and rioting and again the country went into shock and disbelief. News of what was happening was heard around the world. As civil rights leader, Martin Luther King Jr. was well known and respected and his death became a turning point in the fight against racism and racial equality. Over time there was a real change happening and in approximately 40 years racism and racial strife was as low and as good as they had ever been.

Again an assassination attempt was made, this time on President Ronald Reagan; he was shot but survived the attempt and recovered very well. All the extreme ideas and feelings that people have cannot be justified by taking violent action; these ideas and feelings, must be controlled by the individuals through voicing their opinion and exercising restraint.

Although racism will never be completely eliminated, in the years following President Barak Obama's election it has reared it's ugly head to a level unseen in recent history. Individuals such as Pastor Jeremiah Wright were busy stoking the racism fires, encouraging remembrance of past injustices.

The USA has fought wars to gain or maintain freedom at home and abroad. In the early 1990s the gulf war in Iraq, called "Desert Storm", was to reverse the invasion of Kuwait by Iraq. Saddam Hussein wanted Kuwait to have Iraq's huge debts wiped out and have the Kuwait oil and access to the ocean.

Later the (2003 — 2011) next war in Iraq was against terrorism and using weapons of mass destruction. In the 1980ˢ Saddam Hussein used gas for poisoning the Kurdish nationals. Although Saddam Hussein moved through military positions, his reign as president ran from July 1979 until April 2003. Saddam Hussein, a terrible dictator, was deposed and brought to justice, later he was executed for crimes against his own people.

Attacks on the USA, in recent years, have been by terrorists on US soil and embassy compounds around the world. Reasons for the attacks vary from fantastic to real, from "The Devil made me do it!" to "We just hate Americans."

The terrorist organization Al-Qaeda and similar Muslim extremist (terrorist) groups, have claimed credit for the death and destruction caused by these attacks. Many Muslim countries benefit from outrageous amounts of financial support from the US Government/taxpayers, but they don't return the support, or display any loyalty. The USA is always ready to defend the underdog, but has weakened itself by overspending and becoming financially indebted. Now the US Government is very close to a point of no return.

Extremely serious attacks, referred to as the "Nine Eleven" attacks, occurred on September 11th in 2001 and in 2012. Other attacks were made during the years in between. The first attack triggered the war on terrorism and was aimed specifically at the Al-Qaeda terrorist leader, Osama bin Laden.

In the first attack, in less than two hours, more death and destruction was caused by terrorism on US soil than had ever been seen in the history of the United States of America.

Osama bin Laden claimed responsibility. Al-Qaeda and bin Laden blamed US support of Israel, the presence of US troops in Saudi Arabia, and sanctions against Iraq as motives for the attacks. The United States responded to the attacks by launching the "War on Terror" and invading Afghanistan to depose the Taliban, which had harboured Al-Qaeda[20]. Other countries strengthened their anti-terrorism legislation and law enforcement powers. After almost 10 years, Osama bin Laden was located in Pakistan and killed by US forces in May 2011.

The September 11, 2001 attacks resulted in the deaths of 2,996 people, including the 19 hijackers and 2,977 victims. The victims included 246 on the four planes, 2,606 in New York City (in the towers and on the ground), and 125 at the Pentagon. 55 military personnel were among those killed at the Pentagon.

A total of 411 emergency workers died as they tried to rescue people and fight fires. The New York City Fire Department lost 340 firefighters, a chaplain, and two paramedics. The New York City Police Department lost 23 officers. The Port Authority Police Department lost 37 officers. Eight emergency medical technicians and paramedics from private emergency medical services units were killed. [21]

---

20 Nora Fogarty — (recorded Live from 'The Factory,' Nightclub .., http://vimeo.com/69579183 (accessed July 18 2013)

21 September 11 attacks — Wikipedia, the free encyclopedia, http://en.wikipedia.org/wiki/September_11_attacks (accessed July 10 2013)

The Pentagon was severely damaged by the impact of the third plane, causing one section of the building to collapse. Before crashing into the Pentagon, the airplane's wings knocked over light poles and its right engine smashed into a power generator.

After the attacks, the NATO council declared the attacks on the United States were an attack on all NATO nations and affected Article 5 of the NATO charter. This was the first appeal of Article 5, which had been written during the Cold War in anticipation of an attack by the Soviet Union.

The Bush Government declared a war on terror, with goals of bringing bin Laden and Al-Qaeda to justice and preventing an increase of activity in other terrorist groups. This would be accomplished by imposing economic and military sanctions against states sympathetic to terrorist organizations, increasing global surveillance, and intelligence sharing.

In October 2001, the war in Afghanistan began by US and British forces starting aerial bombing campaigns, targeting Taliban and Al-Qaeda camps. Later, the Special Forces invaded Afghanistan with ground troops and other NATO countries joined forces to form a coalition to fight the war on terror.

The overthrow of Taliban rule of Afghanistan, by a US-led coalition, was the second-biggest operation of the US "Global War on Terrorism" outside of the United States, and the largest directly connected to terrorism. Conflict in Afghanistan, between the Taliban insurgency and the International Security Assistance Force, is ongoing.

Many Americans believe that the war in Afghanistan has already cost too many lives and too much money. More and more Americans want their sons and daughters home rather than rebuilding a nation that could be done by the Afghans themselves. Fighting a war, even peacekeeping, is a very difficult task and for soldiers, young men and women of 18 and 19 years and older, it is difficult to maintain objectivity and remain enthusiastic, without that support from home; especially when there is a total lack of gratitude from the Afghan government of Hamid Karzai and other leaders.

The Philippines and Indonesia, as well as other nations with their own internal conflicts with Islamic terrorism, also increased their military readiness.

A detention camp was set up in Cuba as a holding facility for terrorists caught committing acts of terrorism, a nice place for a jail. Of course human rights' groups question the legitimacy of keeping the terrorists on a long vacation and away from their work.

Duh! They are terrorists. They have been allowed to live, which is a luxury *their victims* did not get.

The detention camp in Cuba, Guantanamo Bay, has over the years released some of the inmates, those were not rehabilitated terrorists, the majority are believed to have returned to fighting the 'Jihad' terrorist war.

Much has been written about the horrendous attacks on 9/11/2001 and how the lives of people have been changed forever because of the many lives that were lost. The incident also changed much in our society and our daily lives, such as our sense of security and our suspicion of others around us. Who can we really trust? Air travel costs have gone up, with rates increasing because of added security equipment and personnel.

There is no way that your co-worker is going to be a terrorist and you know the guy next door so well that you would trust him with your wife and kids, really? Have you forgotten the military base shootings or the shipyard shootings, those were done by someone's neighbour and also someone's co-workers.

We're really surprised to find that this nice man next door turned out to be evil or a criminal type.

Don't be surprised his or her life is mostly private and any wrongdoing is not something they are likely to talk about.

Who can you trust, was the question asked after this murderous rampage came to an end. The Fort Hood shootings in November, 2009, were the acts of an army major and psychiatrist; the man shot and killed 13 and wounded 32 more, these were his fellow soldiers. His defense was **his Islamic convictions**.

Then there came the Washington DC Navy shipyard shootings in September, 2013; at least 12 were killed in that attack and his defense claimed he was delusional. There may have been two others involved in those shootings. Then again, maybe not!

Oh no, now we just had another shooting at Fort Hood and the suspect may have had good reason to kill a few others and then himself, his mother had recently passed away, oh sure that makes it so much better to understand. ... When my mother passed away I went and killed at least ... eh ... no one! I just grieved.

Maybe home grown terrorism is on the increase as there have been other cases in recent years, which is making homeland security a very difficult business.

There appears to be an attitude of strife in the world today that doesn't just reveal itself in what goes on in the adult world, but even little kids are bullying others in school and in their nearby neighbourhoods. The schools are almost daily faced with having to deal with bullying students, there is cyber bullying and teens are becoming more violent with each other.

Some twelve or thirteen years ago now, teenagers who were picking on one particular girl just didn't leave her alone, one day they killed her. Reena Virk was severely beaten and drowned by some of her peers, mostly girls and some boys who were involved in this horrible crime. We have all heard reports about bullying that resulted in the targeted person becoming a victim by taking their own life. The peer pressure is so bad that kids commit suicide; it is hard to understand why this is happening.

What is it about hurting other people that seems to be so attractive. The 'knock down game' for instance is not a game when you run up to an unsuspecting person and from behind knock them over to hurt them. It is also not a game when a group of seventy five to a hundred young people run around an area and just indiscriminately attack people. These so called games are hurting and even killing people.

When fighting a war, you know who your enemies are. You can identify them by their uniforms and clothing style. Terrorism is different. It's so vicious. You may be facing a terrorist who is familiar, but not as an enemy.

An assassination attempt was made on the British Ambassador to Libya. The attack took place in Benghazi on June 10, 2012._Many security incidents occurred in Libya between June 2011 and July 2012. Of the 234 incidents 50 took place in Benghazi[22].

The US Consulate, again a target, had explosives detonated outside against the gates of the perimeter wall without causing casualties but incurring a lot of damage.

These attacks alone were reason enough for Ambassador J. Christopher Stevens to request increased security at the U.S. Consulate in Benghazi, Libya, Ambassador J. Christopher Stevens made several such requests only to have them fall on deaf ears.

On September 11, 2012, heavily armed terrorists attacked the United States' Consulate and annex in Benghazi, Libya. The terrorists were armed with rocket-propelled grenades, hand grenades, assault rifles, anti-aircraft machine guns, artillery mounted on trucks, diesel canisters and mortars.

Obviously these guys were not on their way to the local McDonalds.

The group was made up of choice Omar Abdul Rahman Brigades, Ansar Al –Sharia and al-Qaeda fighters, determined to cause as much death, destruction, and pain as they possibly could.

They attacked during the night, at a compound that is meant to protect the consulate building. There was another the next morning. Four people were killed in the two assaults, including U.S. Ambassador J. Christopher Stevens, Information Officer, Sean Smith, and two embassy security personnel, Glen Doherty and Tyrone Woods. Ten others were injured.

---

22 Benghazi Attack — wikipedia, the free encyclopedia, http://en.wikipedia. org/wiki/2012_**Benghazi**_attack (accessed July 12 2013)

After the attack came speeches from the Governments of Libya, the United States, and other countries around the world, with condolences and condemnation of the terrorist action. Blaming a video, "Innocence of Muslims", was a bad move by the US administration—an attempt to try and cover-up the indecision by the State Department to take action at the time of the attacks. It clearly was a premeditated attack by Islamist terrorists.

When US Ambassador J. Christopher Steven's requests for help were denied by, US Secretary of State, despite warnings also by the Libyan President, Hillary Clinton, obviously did not respond properly. There have not been any charges of wrong-doing, but she must be held accountable and ultimately, the Commander in Chief, Barack Obama, also.

The State Department believed that a ten men security team at the CIA compound would be able to assist the consulate during an attack.

A ten-member security team to protect the embassy over a mile away, Protect it against well over 100 irrational terrorists? ... Really??

The terrorists also attacked the CIA compound to complete their mission for the night.

After many conflicting statements, the US President promised to work with the Libyan government to, as he called it, "bring these folks to justice." Now more than a year later no one has been brought to 'justice' yet!

Er ... don't hold your breath folks.

It appears as a game of challenging your allies' loyalty, when you see the way President Obama treats some people, like Israeli Prime Minister Benjamin Netanyahu, Canadian Prime Minister Stephen Harper and Mexico's President Enrique Pena Nieto.

Previous administrations in the White House worked diligently to have good relationships with the leaders of allied countries, but there is something lacking this time around. The promise made to Vladimir Putin by Obama, saying things will be different when I have been re-elected to the White House, we'll get more done, hasn't made a whole lot of difference, except that a comment like that is not inspiring trust in the President.

Vladimir Putin just goes along and does what he wants, like invading Crimea, knowing fine and well that he doesn't have to worry about any interference. He has taken Crimea without firing any shots or spilling blood. East Ukraine will probably be next and I don't think that more stern talks from the White House will be much of a deterrent to Mr. Putin.

When attacked by terrorists, don't give a passive response
Return with a defensive act by striking back.
Don't be weak in your response!

11. Political correctness and alternate lifestyles

Every society needs some form of order: some control; a set of rules to live by; a governing body to keep the peace; and of course, there has to be a reason for politicians to exist!

When the government isn't doing things our way, we have all either said, or heard it said: "I'm not a political animal. I believe in live and let live." The political parties don't seem to know how to get along with each other. The Left is always going after the Right, and the Right is always ~~Wrong~~ right! Well now, that isn't exactly right ... if you know what I mean.

Political correctness has taken on new meaning in the last twenty-five to thirty years. When we went through the Feminist era, a mailman became a mailperson and of course that was carried into every area Women serving on a council became councilperson and so on. But it didn't stop there. Now everyone has to have a good day. You have your car serviced and the service person hands you a bill for $750.00, and tells you to have a good day, he knows fine and well that you're not having a good day, but he is.

Political correctness now means that you can't call a terrorist a "terrorist". You have to call them "violent extremists" or "illegal enemy combatants." This nonsense is going to extremes— violent extremes or (as the colonel used to say) "horse pucky."

Do you ever get irritated at how some things are described, I do and it happens with some little things and also with more significant items. Just to give you an idea, a TV personality tells you that they only deal in facts, but the facts as he calls them are known to be not true, or they correct another person, but the correction is incorrect. My pet peeve is the term 'illegal immigrant'; an immigrant is not illegal but has been accepted officially into a country through an immigration procedure. Someone who enters the country illegally may be called an 'illegal alien,' or an 'illegal,' or a person seeking 'refugee' status, but not immigrant.

Oh, that political correctness is such a nuisance!

It becomes a problem for me when, after a long time, I run into an old friend (for example) and ask him, "How's your wife, what's her name, doing?" That happened to me and I was told, "Huh, I haven't seen her for eleven months now, and that isn't long enough." Why was I embarrassed at such a moment? Was it because I'm too nosey? We used to get together as friends before and had good times together.

When I probed a bit further, I found out that his wife was now living with another woman, and my friend got irritated—not at me, but at the embarrassment of his failed marriage. There was a time when homosexuality was a taboo subject and these things stayed behind closed doors, but that changed quite some time ago.

At first we heard a bit about various people "coming out" and there were gay bashings, but time and again we noticed more publicity being given to the homosexual debate and the morality thereof. Naturally there was the part of the debate that said it was an unnatural act or lifestyle, and then the heated arguments would follow. None of this could justify the behaviour of straight people beating up the gay people or any other bad behaviour.

Slowly, as more joined the ranks of the openly gay community, tolerance for gays and lesbians began to grow, and their lifestyles were being accepted ... or were they?

Personally I have no problem most of the time, but when a friend came over one day and while I was working, leaned over and kissed me, I just about flipped. The excuse was that he had a few too many drinks before he came over, but in my eyes it was totally unacceptable and must never happen again.

In the late nineteen sixties, New York's Greenwich Village was a well-known area for gays and lesbians. The hangout for many was an inn, known to many simply as the "Stonewall." In June of 1969, the police (armed with a warrant) raided the place. Liquor was being served on the premises, and as the Stonewall was without a license, the place was closed legally. This effectively put an end to the gay scene at the Stonewall. It was a very real gay community in 1969, and very well known, but it was by no means the only one. This was not the end of the gay community, or the gay lifestyle. If it had been, the gay rights movement would not have grown to where it is today.

With large numbers of cities and communities around the country celebrating gay pride days, and hosting gay pride parades, and (more recently) accepting gay marriages, homosexuality is definitely not a behind-closed-doors issue any longer.

Over the years, since the Stonewall incident, many men and women have publicly announced their homosexuality, including celebrities and public officials. Even an official of the United Nations, Secretary General Ban Ki-moon, has spoken out and voiced support for the rights of the homosexuals and for gay marriage—calling on world nations to repeal their bigoted legislations against homosexual people.

In a statement, Secretary General Ban Ki-moon called for a repeal of laws that criminalize gay marriages in countries around the world. He also called on the countries to curb violence against homosexual, bisexual, and transgender people, decriminalize same-sex relationships, ban prejudice, and educate the public.

Of course, Secretary General Ban Ki-moon got criticized for using the UN as an outlet to express his personal opinions, even though all the religions, including Christianity, Judaism, Islam, etc., oppose the idea of same-sex marriage.

During an African Union summit, UN Secretary General Ban Ki-moon urged the African leaders to respect gay rights in Africa. In an exclusive, televised interview with the mainstream ABC network, US President Barack Obama also announced his outright support for same-sex marriage. "At a certain point, I've just concluded that, for me personally, it is important to go ahead and affirm that I think same-sex couples should be able to get married."

Meanwhile, according to mainstream American media outlets, Obama advisers say that he had intended to publicize his position on same-sex marriage before the Democratic Party officially nominated him for re-election in September—for campaign purposes.

Uh huh! Uh hUh!

There are several symbols and flags that are used in LGBT activities, such as the pink and black triangle, worn on inmate clothing in German concentration and death camps during WW2.

Interesting that symbols, that were symbols of shame, by the Nazis, were chosen by people who are wishing to remove associated shame from their lifestyles.

It's one thing to be tolerant of alternative lifestyles, though it's another to have the LGBT group working to change the definition of an age-old institution like marriage.

Studies conducted in several countries indicate that support for the legalization of same-sex marriage increases with higher levels of education and that support is strong among younger people. Additionally, polls show that there is rising support for same-sex marriage across all races, ages, religions, socioeconomic statuses, etc.. The study could be biased. In any case, it suggests that young people, and those with higher levels of education, support gay marriage.[23]

Am I uneducated and old? I have several friends in the gay and lesbian community. I also have a lesbian niece and a gay nephew. They mean a lot to me, I love them but I don't agree with their way of life. both have had various partners but do not plan to marry. They would be free to marry, living in Holland, the first country to legalize same sex marriage.

---

23 Same Sex Marriage — Wikipedia, the free encyclopedia, http://en.wikipedia.org/wiki/Same-sex_marriage (accessed May 15 2013)

As reported on The Blaze:

January 28, 2013 on The Blaze TV, Glenn Beck reported a news item from CNN.com about the Boy Scouts' organization and potential liberalization of its standards;

BREAKING NEWS
CNN.com Jan. 28 2013

Boy Scouts' spokesman says organization is discussing "potentially removing" membership restriction on sexual orientation. [24]

The Blaze TV

It is clear that, wherever we go, there are gays and lesbians. It is also clear that there are customs and traditions that are specific to different regions and countries of the world. For centuries, local authority has ruled based on their own customs and traditions. No outside organization should come in and push their "one size fits all" policies on those local authorities. The UN may not interfere in the domestic affairs of any country.

Recently I had a bad night, in fact I didn't sleep for hours, worried about my own political correctness; did I measure up, did I really make the grade? Living in a bi-lingual country comes with a certain amount of responsibilities and it shows up everywhere. On the products in the grocery store both languages are printed and on the toys in the toy store, instructions are always carefully bi-lingual, even on the official

---

24   Boy Scouts' sexual orientation – CNN.com Jan.28 2013/The Blaze TV Jan.28 2013 (accessed Jan 28 2013)

government publications both languages are printed; call a federal government office and you are greeted with a cheerful "bon-jour."

As I said earlier, I didn't sleep very well and for good reason, I had not given this political correctness topic enough thought myself, I had not considered that in this book there has to be attention paid to the language that is used. My goodness, after all, if we are to get the kind of education that addresses the concerns of all our people in this multi cultural society we must make sure that we cover every aspect of this important subject.

Hier moet ik aller eerst mijn verontschuldiging aanbieden want ik hebt dat tot noch toe niet gedaan. Waarom spreeken wij in het Hollands terwijl we het in het Frans moeten doen?

Oops, I must not have flipped the right switch? The French language switch that is.

Style de Vie croquants a l'avoine avec canneberges et agrumes, solution de vie! A la sauce a sauter en remuant! …..
Pardonney moi mon ami…pardon my French, it is bad *nonh* ?

Halloo, this is not being politically correct as it becomes almost insulting without knowing or having proper command of the language. French is not an easy language to learn. I know from experience that different languages are spoken all around us from which we may pick up words and phrases, but speaking a language fluently and writing it correctly is much more difficult.

How politically correct should we be?
Always be polite but don't lie about your convictions.

12. Fair trade versus redistribution of the Wealth

In recent years there has been a strong move in our society to bring a balance in trading practices. This is primarily aimed at trading with developing countries to provide fair prices to the producers for their goods and encourage consistent quality of the products. These fair trade products are sold to us at only slightly higher prices than average priced products.

My real fair trade experience came while living on the prairies, where during harvest time, able bodies are put to work with the harvesting activities. It was a learning process for a city slicker like myself, not knowing anything about farm life. Harvest time allows no room for relaxing; every waking hour is precious, and you soon learn what to do and how to do it. The farmer I learned from was a forgiving kind of guy, and my errors were no problem to him. For instance, we were stacking bales of hay, and in my eagerness, I stacked them one row too high. Hey, when I fell off the truck onto my head, it didn't bother him at all. He even let me take a coffee break before I had to finish the job.

For me, the real payoff came in the form of food—real food. He took me duck hunting on his farm and I could keep as many ducks as I could shoot. I'm not sure if this trade would have passed in today's fair-trade environment. Somehow this prairie life seemed okay, but I was looking for a more balanced trade. One of my new friends invited me to go deer hunting. There would be two other fellows on the hunt. I thought it was a great idea—better than getting a bunch of ducks for three bruised ribs. My friend had an old army jeep that could take us deep into the hunting areas, where the average car would not be able to go.

The fourth man in the hunting party was our key to success. A friend of my friend, he was a local Cree Indian who had been a hunter since he was a youngster.

When we got to Roy's house he was just about ready. The foresight of his rifle was missing though, so he cut the head off a nail, a quarter inch down the stem, and stuck the nail head down into the sight groove. A tin can in the yard proved to be a good target, and so it became the first victim. He was almost ready now, but asked if we could wait till he had lifted his nets, which he used for ice fishing—something I had never tried. So then we went to some lake. It turns out, when ice-fishing, you drive the jeep onto the lake to get to where the ice-fishing hole is.

Is the ice that strong? And what about the fish? After some ice was chopped out of the hole, we helped Roy retrieve his nets. There were many big, white fish and (with socks on our hands) we removed them from the nets and dropped them onto the ice surface. They soon stopped moving and were quick-frozen on the spot. Back again we went to Roy's house.

Okay, we were almost ready now, but Roy had to get some firewood for his house. So we helped him cut some firewood. Well, that was great. Then we all got in the jeep—rifles and hunting gear ready—and away we went. After about a mile or two, Roy told the driver to go left onto the next road. The snow was fairly fresh, but in that fine jeep we would still be able to go deeper into the woods.

"Road coming up," Roy warned, and there it was. Turning onto this road, we split the difference of the left turn and skidded off the road. No problem. We had a four-wheel-drive jeep. Yeah right. The four wheels started digging and we went deeper and deeper. Then we hung up, straddling a log, with no wheels on solid anything.

While assessing the situation, Roy noticed something moving. It was far away, so we followed him a ways as he quietly walked. Then he stopped. "There are two," he said softly. "You take the left," he said, nodding towards me, and then to my friend, "and you take the right."

Simple enough, but before any shots were fired, the deer started moving again. "Bang! Bang!"

Just like that, both deer dropped. "You guys too slow," Roy said. He had dropped them both before anyone even got a shot off. Great balls of fire! "Let's go get the deer, and then try and get the jeep out!"

On my way home that evening, with two big, frozen fish and a chunk of deer meat, I began to see the picture a bit clearer. It may have been the warmth of my car, but there seemed to be a bit more of a balance in the day's toils. It was certainly a learning experience. There was still more work to be done before I could brag about fair trade!

The Fair Trade Movement does not explain how much extra is charged for fair trade goods, or how much of that extra price reaches the producer. Use of the fair trade brand has gone far beyond food and goods—a development that has been par-ticularly vibrant in Great Britain, where there are many fair trade towns, fair trade universities, fair trade churches, and fair trade schools. Well, that's Great Britain! That seems fair enough!

My neighbour was a coffee buyer for a large US company, and spent many years in the "trade." His reaction to the Fair Trade Movement was to say, "I could not do business if it wasn't fair for my suppliers and producers."

Fair trade seems to be a serious strategy by various countries and organizations to be just that—Fair in trade—but they need to keep the United Nations out of it. It is working quite well. Keep it that way!

Re-Distribution of the wealth

With a good income, a person can live well but not be wealthy. With lots of assets a person may be wealthy, but have an average income. If your liabilities equal your assets, you're broke!

This principle applies to countries as well, for instance the US is a very wealthy country but so deeply in debt that going broke is almost inevitable. Owing money to lenders creates an obligation that must be met. This situation is caused by overspending and careless management of finances; in other words spending money in excess of your income.

In an effort to bring equality to the masses, governments will redistribute wealth by taking tax money to provide for the poor and needy.

There is however a danger of abuse in the welfare systems. Effective control of proper use of such systems is not that easily attained.

When Reality Hits

Recently I watched Mr. Watters (Watters' World) do an interview with a young man in California; he is a surfer and plays a guitar. In a segment of the interview, it showed him doing some food shopping which included a Lobster.

Mr. Watters asked him how he supported himself, to which the surfer answered; welfare and food stamps, the system works fine. The system is set up for me to be able to live this way. The interviewer then asked, "don't you feel guilty that you are taking advantage of people? It is their tax that pays for your lifestyle, why don't you get a job?" The surfer dude replied, "I have a job, I am a musician in a band." "How much does that earn you," the interviewer asked, the answer was "well we haven't received any money yet."

A short time later, surfer dude was interviewed yet again, this time in a television studio by Sean Hannity. The same attitude was clearly there, he feels that he is entitled to government support. When Sean Hannity asked him if a job was offered him that would pay $80,000—per year would he move to take the job, his answer was no! Entitlement mentality shows up even at the beach.

Redistribution of wealth is not based on Fairness.

Remember what I told you about my grandmother: When my grandfather died, the local authorities made my grandmother give up more than half of her home so that a police detective and his wife could move in and occupy the other part. Her housekeeper had to go, because there was not enough room for living quarters for her. This was not a voluntary move for my grandmother. She also did not get proper compensation for losing the use of half of her house.

The United States has opted for the redistribution of wealth and ultimately socialism. Each of these programs provides services or financial aid to those called poor, as defined by the government.

NOTE: A general misconception about class is that, if you are wealthy or have a lot of money, you are the upper class, and if you are not wealthy or have a low income, you are a lower class. That is not true. Class is **not** related to money. It is about character, integrity, uprightness, and behaviour.

When working hard to earn a good income and some of that income is taken from you in taxes, is given to someone else, it is being redistributed through welfare or food stamps toward income equality. When you have worked much harder and longer for your earnings, that type of income equality has no fairness in it.

For example, when in a college class exam there are grades given to all the participants which will vary from good to bad and you apply the redistribution of wealth principle, then all the participants will be equal.

Let's assume out of twenty-five participants:

three got 100 points   seven got 70 points   three got 55 points
four got 45 points   six got 30 points   two got 15 points
Total 1345 points

By redistributing the exam participants' wealth (1345 points) Divided by 25 = 53.8 points

The score of 53.8 points is barely a passing grade and this system hardly an incentive to work around the clock for higher scores.

Redistribution of wealth is a basic principle of the socialist ideology. It takes from those who have, in order to give to those who have not, and does so in order to balance things. The main flaw in that philosophy is that charity must be voluntary, not forced by authority.

Fairness in trade should also apply at home.

But stop the redistribution of wealth.

13. Global warming

Are we faced with a catastrophic situation of global proportions or are we faced with deceptive stories not based on honest scientific research and truth?

As reported by "The Foundry"
Climate Talks or Wealth Redistribution Talks?
Nicolas Loris
November 19, 2010 at 11:55 am

Typically the largest wealth distribution program that occurs in Cancun, Mexico, is college students spending their parents' money. That could change at the upcoming United Nations climate summit if developing countries clamoring for money to cope with global warming get their wish. With each passing year, it's clear that international climate change talks are less about climate and more about wealth redistribution.

The latest case in point comes from United Nations Intergovernmental Panel on Climate Change (IPCC) official Ottmar Edenhofer. In a recent interview with Germany's NZZ Online,

Edenhofer lays out just what the climate talks are all about:

NZZ: The new thing about your proposal for a Global Deal is the stress on the importance of development policy for climate policy. Until now, many think of aid when they hear development policies.

Edenhofer: That will change immediately if global emission rights are distributed. If this happens, on a per capita basis, then Africa will be the big winner, and huge amounts of money will flow there. This will have enormous implications for development policy. And it will raise the question if these countries can deal responsibly with so much money at all.

NZZ: That does not sound anymore like the climate policy that we know.

Edenhofer: Basically it's a big mistake to discuss climate policy separately from the major themes of globalization. The climate summit in Cancun at the end of the month is not a climate conference, but one of the largest economic conferences since the Second World War. Why? Because we have 11,000 gigatons of carbon in the coal reserves in the soil under our feet—and we must emit only 400 gigatons in the atmosphere if we want to keep the 2-degree target. 11,000 to 400—there is no getting around the fact that most of the fossil reserves must remain in the soil.

NZZ: De facto, this means an expropriation of the countries with natural resources. This leads to a very different development from that which has been triggered by development policy.

Edenhofer: First of all, developed countries have basically expropriated the atmosphere of the world community. But one must say clearly that we redistribute de facto the world's wealth by climate policy. Obviously, the owners of coal and oil will not be enthusiastic about this. One has to free oneself from the illusion that international climate policy is environmental policy. This has almost nothing to do with environmental policy anymore, with problems such as deforestation or the ozone hole.

This shouldn't be all too surprising. The Copenhagen conference last year quickly devolved from a discussion on how to cost-effectively curtail greenhouse gas emissions—the primary culprit behind global warming, according to the U.N.—into a browbeating session designed to get developed countries to accept massive economic costs arising from carbon dioxide cuts and to provide billions of dollars in wealth transfers (up to $100 billion annually was discussed in Copenhagen last year) to help developing nations cope with the projected consequences of a changing climate. Meanwhile, developing countries (even the large developing country emitters like India and China) were being exempted from emissions restrictions even though that would undermine any possibility of meeting emissions targets.

Last year in Copenhagen, Janos Pasztor, the director of U.N. Secretary-General Ban Ki-moon's Climate Change Support Team, admitted: "This is not a climate-change negotiation. ... It's about something much more fundamental. It's about economic strength." The nations at the negotiation, he added, "just have to slug it out."

It goes to show how ill-suited the United Nations is at handling a climate treaty. The competing interests of U.N. member states make it extremely difficult for the negotiations not to get sidetracked.

In the end, there is a reason why these conferences are often held in exotic locales. But instead of college kids spending their parents' money on spring break, it's international diplomats spending our taxpayer dollars on conferences focused on how to they can spend even more down the road. [25]

Nicolas Loris

Now doesn't that make you feel warm all over? Our man from the UN is telling us, "We fooled you and you were dumb enough to fall for it!"

It's amazing to me that, through an organization founded to keep the peace amongst its member nations, we (in an underhanded way) have been drawn into globalization. What's next? A New World Order?

UN-believable! Global Redistribution of Wealth

The United Nations is continuing its assault on American wealth and sovereignty. Unbelievably, various proposals are in the works to tax American citizens and send the money to poorer countries with the blessings of the president.

The threat has become so serious that delegates to the Republican National Convention have adopted a proposal rejecting the United Nations' efforts to tax Americans. Now, preserving American freedom and keeping tax dollars in America is to be an official part of the conservative platform.

President Obama and extreme liberals in Congress are supportive of these various UN efforts, of course, and that is a big

---

25

Climate Talks or Wealth Redistribution Talks? | The Foundry .., http://Blog.
heritage.org/2010/11/19/climate-talks-or-wealth-redistribution-talks/
(accessed July 18   2013)

reason why the conservatives are finding it necessary to come out against any and all efforts at global wealth redistribution.

Yes, global wealth redistribution. Liberal Governments are roping us into giving up what we have worked for, by supporting the UN proposals and taking actions that are by no means democratically achieved. If you didn't like the way Obamacare (the Affordable Care Act) taxes came into being, think about the next bunch of taxes that are on the horizon. As long as countries support the UN, an organization that doesn't stick to its own rules, who knows what might be next?

Like Egypt, Libya, and Iran, just to mention a few of the countries that are getting the benefits of those tax dollars from you. They are doing wonderful things. The President even hands out gifts of planes, tanks, and money to other countries ... but not at home. He's robbing his own people blind.

Although the United States of America already funds approximately 22% of the UN, they are simply not satisfied. America could lose its sovereignty; the economic situation could worsen significantly. The Congressional Budget Office issued a report earlier this year stating that just the transactions' tax alone could kill jobs and undermine America's role as the dominant financial power in the world.

Many times I have made reference to the UN, and not always in the most flattering ways. My concern is that many people have become involved in the UN organization, and as such, have lost sight of its principles. The scandals that have occurred may have various reasons, but none of them are justified or should be excused.

Talking about scandals is not a popular subject, and of course, that is not my intention in writing this book. However, I'm talking about reality. During my younger years, during the last century, there was a real problem of white slavery in Europe, with young white girls being kidnapped and sold into Middle East harems. Similarly, young men were being kidnapped or tricked into signing up for the French Foreign Legion—my cousin among them.

There is modern-day slavery as well, and I'm not talking about what my wife refers to when she talks about me being a slave driver. This is the real thing and very serious! Real slavery in Mauritania, bad you say? It gets worse. The UN is aware of it and turns a blind eye!

As reported by the National Post:

> Tom Gross, National Post | 25/02/13 |
> Last Updated: 22/02/13 2:41 PM ET
>
> Geneva Summit
> Tom Gross.
> The UN's willful ignorance of modern-day
> slavery in Mauritania
>
> The UN Human Rights Council (UNHRC) begins
> its annual session in Geneva today by once
> again disgracing itself through the appointment
> of the West African country of Mauritania as its
> vice-president for the next year.
>
> The UNHRC is the organization that, in the
> past, has cozied up to the Gaddafi and Assad
> regimes in Libya and Syria; that praised Sri

Lanka's human-rights record shortly after that country's military killed more than 40,000 Tamil civilians; and that still exhibits at the entrance to its meeting hall, two pieces of art, one donated by Egypt's Mubarak regime, the other with a plaque that reads, "A statue of Nemesis, Goddess of justice, donated by the Syrian government."

It also appointed Alfred De Zayas as one of its leading advisors last December, despite the fact that his books on the Second World War portray Germans as victims and the Allies as perpetrators of "genocide." De Zayas, while not denying the Holocaust himself, has nonetheless become a hero to many Holocaust deniers, and his sayings are featured on many of their websites. He has called for Israel to be expelled from the UN, while defending the ruthless Iranian regime.

NOTE: *Alfred-Maurice De Zayas is a Cuban born American human rights lawyer and UNHRC official.*

And now Mauritania has been chosen by the UNHRC to help preside over worldwide human rights for the next 12 months. Mauritania, although all-but ignored by mainstream human-rights groups, is a country that allows

20% of its citizens, about 800,000 people, some as young as 10, to live as slaves.

An estimated 27 million people worldwide still live in conditions of forced bondage, and every year at least 700,000 people are trafficked across borders and into slavery, according to figures compiled by the U.S. State Department, the International Organization for Migration and other reliable sources.

But nowhere is slavery still so systematically practiced as in Mauritania, an Islamic republic where imams often use their interpretations of Sharia law to justify forcing the darker-skinned black African Haratine minority to serve as slaves to the Arabic Moor population.

"The situation is every bit as bad as it was in apartheid South Africa, and in many ways it is worse," Abidine Merzough, the European coordinator for the anti-slavery NGO Initiative for the Resurgence of the Abolitionist Movement in Mauritania, told the fifth annual Geneva Summit for Human Rights and Democracy last week.

"Officially, the Mauritanian authorities have abolished slavery on five separate occasions. But in reality, it exists exactly as before, backed up by imams and other clergy who write laws and issue fatwas justifying slavery," said Merzough, who was born to slaves in Mauritania but is a rare example of someone who managed to escape and now lives in Germany.

"Slaves are their masters' property, often from birth. Women slaves are allowed to be sexually abused whenever their masters want. The masters can buy or sell slaves or loan out parts of their bodies for use — arms, legs, vaginas, mouths. The slaves must obey. This is Islamic law as it exists in Mauritania today," Merzough told the Geneva Summit, which (to their credit) was this year attended by a small number of UNHRC ambassadors from democratic countries (including Canada).

Last year I attended both the Geneva Summit and the opening session of the UN Human Rights Council. The contrast could hardly be greater. I watched the UN ambassadors arrive in chauffeur-driven Mercedes, and then congratulate themselves while ignoring human-rights' abuses throughout the world. The Geneva Summit, by comparison, is put together on a very modest budget by 20 NGOs, headed by UN Watch, an organization that does such good work for human-rights issues that the UNHRC should hang its head in shame.

"Mauritanian law allows masters to buy or sell slaves or loan out parts of their bodies. The slaves must obey" — Abidine Merzough

At this year's Geneva Summit, I moderated a panel that included Mukhtar Mai, an extraordinarily brave woman who was gang raped on the order of a tribal court in Pakistan after it was alleged (wrongly) that her brother had acted immodestly. And after the rape, instead of committing suicide (which is common after such experiences in Pakistan), she has fought a 10 year legal battle in an effort to bring the perpetrators to justice.

Other speakers at this year's Geneva summit included dissidents, torture survivors and witnesses from Congo, Iran, Tibet, Syria, North Korea and elsewhere — as well as Pyotr Verzilov, the husband of the jailed lead singer of the Russian band Pussy Riot

When Britain's Foreign Secretary, William Hague, and other dignitaries assemble in Geneva to open the annual session of the UNHRC today, they might want to ask why these dissidents were not invited to address them. And they might want to ask why Mauritania, instead of being held to account,

has been appointed the organization's vice-
chair. [26] — National Post

Tom Gross is a former foreign correspondent of the London
Sunday Telegraph.

Obviously there is a lot lacking where compassion is concerned, but what goes much deeper is the sense of power
that officials seem to project. Perceived or real misuse of
power is a real concern.

Being critical of some business competitors, we might
define a "consultant" as a guy with a briefcase 100 miles from
home. The concern, though, is very real when unqualified
people are promoted or appointed to positions of responsibility and power goes to their heads; trouble is soon to follow.
The job now becomes an excuse for certain luxuries and lifestyle without accountability.

The Global Warming movement and the truth.

In the late 1980s, there were people with concerns about an
increase in global temperatures. This was the reason they
started talking about global warming.

When I read what the scientists have to say on this subject,
I realize that it's hard to be convinced that we'll be growing
coconuts at the North Pole in the near future. That the CO2
levels from human population contribution is likely to have
an enormous impact on the way the global temperatures will

---

26 Tom Gross: The UN's willful ignorance of modern-day slavery .., http://
beforeitsnews.com/eu/2013/02/tom-gross-the-uns-willful-ignorance-of-
modern-day-slavery-2510036.html (accessed July 20 2013)

go up or down seems rather dubious, but let's see what else science has to tell us.

Studies involving ice-drilling in Antarctica and Greenland demonstrate that a rise in carbon dioxide levels in the atmosphere follows the rise of global temperatures by several centuries. A careful scientific analysis of ice core records over 650,000 years demonstrates that global temperature increases have preceded rather than followed increases in CO2.

Let me repeat that. Rising levels of carbon dioxide follow higher global temperatures. The oceans, which cover 70 percent of the earth's surface, contain more than fifty times the amount of carbon dioxide that exist in the atmosphere. There is a constant interchange between the oceans and the atmosphere of CO2 (approximately every five years). Carbon dioxide is more soluble in cold water than in warm water. When the oceans warm, the water releases much more carbon dioxide into the atmosphere. However when the oceans cool, they absorb much more carbon dioxide. For comparison, bear in mind that a warm carbonated beverage has more fizz than a cold one. It turns out that global temperature actually determines and controls the level of carbon dioxide in the atmosphere and not the other way around.[27]

Now that is very interesting, especially when the likes of Al Gore seem to be doing their best to convince anyone who

---

27 The Global- Warming Deception: How a Secret Elite Plans to Bankrupt America ... Grant R. Jeffrey (by permission from Water Brook Press/Penguin Random House)

will listen that the icebergs and glaciers are going to melt and flood coastal areas, etc..

The Anthropogenic Global Warming (AGW) crowd also talks about more taxes, laws, and restrictions, such as:

- large cars (except Al Gore's)
- levy Eco tax on cars entering the City

- electricity (smart meters)
- permits to drive your car outside your City

- own a second car / -own second home
- ban families from vacationing by car

- limit your choices of buying appliances
- new babies / forced family planning

- garbage
- holiday airline fares

- issue carbon credits (annual limits)
- incandescent light bulbs

- ban bottled water
- ban plasma televisions

- ban private cars from some areas
- ban electric hot water systems

- ban three day weekends that encourage vacation travel
- remove white lines from roads to make motorists drive more carefully
- ban open fires, wood burning and coal burning stoves
- ban new airports and expansion of existing ones
- ban "standby" mode on appliances (remote control)
- ban coal fired electric power generation

When Reality Hits

These things aren't very funny. Right now we must fight to stop greedy and immoral bureaucrats at the UN from getting their hands on more money. Most of us can do without the problems of global warming or more accurately "Climate Change." But to have everything changed, restricted, or banned is an absolute outrage, and again, it's being done by the aggressive characters of "The New World Order."

Global warming or not
We should do our part to protect our environment.

14. Why bother to vote?

The most recent election campaigns in America and Canada have become like Barnum & Bailey Circus performances, and at times could be seen as reminiscent of TV Wrestling bouts. It makes you wonder if politicians also have to be members of the Actors Guild.

Indeed why bother to vote? Well, it wasn't always like that.

In the late fifties, before I came to North America, voting was compulsory. If we didn't vote, we would be faced with a fine. It was our duty!

In North America, it is a privilege to be able to vote and choose a person you can believe in. No matter how careful we are, we can end up with a change we didn't want! Well now, I don't want to get political, after all we do need freedom of choice. But that is what voting is all about—using your vote/ voice to promote someone you believe in—someone who represents you and the party principles you hold dear.

Something I wish could change about America is the time taken for campaigning. Let's face it, there are years wasted campaigning while there is pressing business to attend to. Millions of dollars get spent on all this hoopla and then people are still changing their minds the day before the elections. There should be a time limit of say two to six months, and a maximum amount of money to be spent, on the federal campaign—similar to both the state and municipal or the pro-vincial and municipal election campaigns. People elect and pay their politicians to do the job of governing, *not* the job of campaigning. Therefore, politicians must do *that* on their own time, spending a limited but set amount of their *own* money.

Presidential elections are for a four-year term, with a maximum of two terms, for a total of 8 years.

Senate elections are every 2 years in a 3-classes system. One third is renewed every 2 years, total term 6 years' each. House of Representatives' elections are also held every 2 years on the first Tuesday after November 1st in even years correlating with presidential or half through presidential terms.

State elections are held, by many states, at the same time as the presidential elections. Governors are elected; in most states the elections are held at the same time as the federal elections but a few states hold their elections during odd-numbered years.

Local government, (municipal) are county and city govern-ment. Their elections vary from jurisdiction to jurisdiction and their election dates will also vary.

Oh how I hate hearing the news reporters telling us that the polls are light, so it must be because of the rain. It's your privilege to vote. Remember that if you don't, you cannot complain when your guy doesn't get the job and you're stuck with the other schmuck!

History tells us that voting for a change in government administration is what incumbent politicians would like to promote in order to gain a new position. Often they cannot accomplish what was promised. Sometimes empty promises are made on purpose with no intention to deliver and that has earned politicians the dubious reputation of not being trustworthy.

We also know that elections can be plagued by "voter fraud" and that causes the wrong party, not the true choice of the people, to win. Voter fraud is not easily sorted out and no matter what the results are, it leaves many people distrusting the winning party. These types of voter crimes are often a precursor to the establishment of a dictatorship.

This concern for voter fraud has become a reason for extra precaution by having auditors or monitors present at polling stations, registering with personal identification before using a ballot and very limited deviation from the procedure. Unfortunately personal identification before registering and using a ballot is not used in the US Federal elections and the onus is on individual trust, this is wide open to abuse.

The distrust of the election process has various countries call on other neutral and trusted countries provide supervision during an election day, now also a United Nations' involvement.

Political process, no matter at what level of government, is a needed process to make the various governments work. *A loaded statement, yes but true just the same!* We elect our politicians because we believe that they represent us, and present our beliefs at all three levels of government. That is how it works. Those who are elected are faced with difficult work, representing many people of varying backgrounds—all with their own priorities and ideas. I believe in party policies. That is why party principles and policies are very important in politics—a clear statement or 'platform' made by the party that a politician is a member of, and therefore represents and acts for.

The US Democratic Party removed any reference to God from their platform during the 2012 election campaign but after a public outcry replaced it again.

Politicians are needed to represent us and govern, and they need our support to do so. Unfortunately, the politician needs to be spotless in behaviour and in practising their profession, and that brings about some serious situations. This, for some, is a problem, mostly because of the power of the position and the money involved in the business being conducted.

US Federal election dates are set and do not vary across the country. Canadian Federal or Provincial elections on the other hand may be called before their term is up. Municipal election dates are set and do not change.

Party policy is always a starting point in the search for a party to choose when elections are held. The presentation of party policies is quite often obscure while a politician is in the midst of campaigning.

The wild promises that are made often are not even in line with policy. The eager candidate will sometimes lose perspective of the principles in the quest of winning. Beware!

A democratic system allows the public's opinion to be heard and acted on by the governing party. This is the basic principle of a democracy, but if the policy of the democratic system is not followed, i.e. not sticking to the constitution for instance, the democracy is no longer. Than any ideology may creep into the system and basic control may be lost. This type of situation lends itself to abuse of power and to a dictatorship of some sort, not such a desirable prospect.

A definitive reason to vote and make your wishes known, your vote counts.

When choosing a politician to vote for, the first thing I check out is the party he or she is a member of. Does that party share my values, and are its policies or platform in line with what I believe? The next thing I check out would have to be the personal reputation and working record of the politician. The charisma of the politician is not what I should be voting for. Can he or she do a good job in representing me, my needs, and my beliefs? Some politicians are voted in on their charisma and personal appeal, instead of their character or past record ... and often this becomes disappointing.

So much for my rants, but remember:

It's our privilege and right to vote — use it or lose it!

NOTE: Canadian elections seem much simpler. Party leaders are chosen by members while attending their party's leadership convention. Each party supports their eligible nominees during a five-week campaign, and then people vote. After the election, the leader of the winning party becomes Prime Minister. The election process takes about two months to accomplish.

Vote when you can voice your opinion,
Choose your leaders, vote, whenever eligible vote!

15. This is not going to happen here!

Nature gives us a perfect picture of life; when there is an abundant food supply, a lot of wildlife will live in harmony, but if you change the food supply and everything is on edge, the hunter becomes the hunted and all are on high alert. This is a clear picture for how most of us are in life.

We have been blessed with an amazing variety of wildlife, and I never get tired of seeing deer, moose, elk, bear, mountain goats, cougar, and lynx. Around my home, I see eagles, rabbits, raccoons, squirrels, and various game birds. We also enjoy seeing seals, sea lions, dolphins, killer whales, and a variety of other whales when we're out on the water trying to catch a few fish or just spending the day sailing.

There was a time, when our kids were small, that my hunting would supply food for the family. I could walk across the road from our home, into some trees at the edge of an alfalfa field, and pick off enough rabbits for a few days of delicious fresh meat. On one such an occasion, I was surprised by a large bear, eating berries. He surprised me, as he suddenly stood up, but I surprised him also. He was about 45 or maybe 50 feet away from me, and my reaction was to shoot at him. Hunting rabbits requires a very small and not so powerful bullet—a .22 short is fine. The bear, however ...Wow. I hit him on the forehead and this little piece of lead just bounced off.

He growled and took off running. I also took off, but in the opposite direction ... just in case he changed his mind.

Traditionally, our natives have been credited with being great hunters, and I learned first hand that it is true. However, there is always an exception. There was a certain amount of bartering for goods that went on when we lived on the prairies. It worked out well for us. We kept a freezer well stocked with food that way, and it helped take up the slack when money was tight. One day, I bartered for a large pig, with the butchering included. This filled the freezer right up and I still had the pig's head in the trunk of my car. Considering the winter weather, the car trunk acted just like another freezer.

My friend Emma sent me a message, saying that she needed me. So I went to the reserve to see her. Emma's father was in the hospital, about sixty miles away, and she really wanted to go see him. Could I take her? We arranged a time for me to pick her up, and planned to spend a day on her visit. When I went to pick her up, there was Emma with three other family members—all fairly heavy ladies, and one of whom had a suitcase. Seeing my passengers, I suggested that the suitcase should go in the trunk. Upon opening the trunk, Emma looked at the pig's head and asked quietly, "Oh, you have been hunting?"

Sometime later, Emma invited me for dinner, which was a kind gesture on her part. While visiting before dinner, I could see the cooking pot on the wood stove, and more importantly, I could see what was in the cooking pot. There it was: a beaver with some of its teeth hanging over the edge of the pot, while the Bannock was baking on another part of the stove. That experience put a whole new twist on fine country dining.

Back in my younger days, my friend's father, Mr. Budecq, had a shoe factory that produced quality handmade shoes, and his loyal employees were fine tradesmen who worked for him with pride. The company was run efficiently and the products were fairly priced. But along came the government and took over the factory, saying that they would improve production. Mr. Budecq was allowed to be a worker in his own factory, which now belonged to the federal government.

We would never fall prey to that, or to Ponzi schemes, bank bailouts, industries failing, or governments taking over segments of the private sector industries ... or would we?

Let's see ... there was Bernard Madoff. He was definitely among the worst Ponzi scheme crooks that we know of. Banks and financial institutions too big to fail, and auto industries and solar energy companies all in good health after the government bailouts? Check it out. The results may be disappointing.

Maybe the President felt sorry for those bank executives and CEOs in big industry. Maybe this really was an act of kindness from his heart. Taxpayers are really good in providing spending money for the President and his cronies, but unfortunately many of those taxpayers lost their jobs and their homes, as the banks had mismanaged the mortgages and the banking business. They gave mortgages to people who really could not afford the payments, and then (when problems arose) the banks had no idea who the current mortgage holders were, as they had sold mortgages by the truckload to foreign investors. These were almost criminal business practices.

In a "Social Democracy" there is a great future for a failing business, because (after all) the government stands ready to take the business and pour money (so much money!) into it. This extends the life of the top management and provides more opportunities for them to get big bonuses, before leaving the "sinking ship" altogether and starting a new venture. The bailout money and those big bonuses, well I have a feeling there might have been enough money to pay off a lot of mortgages, preserving numerous family homes, and preventing much misery.

America's had its share of government bailouts in recent years, and it appears that the recipients have not been able to improve their business practices significantly. There are rumours of more bailouts being needed. Granted, some of the banks didn't need or want a bailout, and even in the auto industry, not all were in need of rescue by the Feds, but most were. Is government set up to own and operate those various companies that received billions of dollars? If our governments are becoming involved in the private sector, by bailing out failing businesses and even taking over control, then we are faced with serious problems.

Will government come in and take over our companies, telling us that they are going to improve productivity and then allowing us to work in what used to be our own businesses, like my friend's father, Mr. Budecq?

The Feds may make certain moves that are unpopular, but as long as they are legal moves, people really have very little power to protect or defend themselves. Talking about defending ourselves, do you own a gun? If it is a legally bought and owned gun, then you may be in trouble. Depending on where you live, the local gun control nuts might soon be sending the police or sheriff to your door asking you to give up your gun.

Wow, for a fleeting moment, I thought it was an effort by the Feds to take the guns away from private citizens to beef up the military forces after all the budget cuts they have had to endure. However, I have been reassured that the idea was just a bit paranoid. Everyone is fine with the budget cuts for the military.

Just think! I was being paranoid! And I was thinking! I know. That's dangerous. But hey, wait a minute ... you're taking my gun anyway? Why? It's mine! Here is my permit and the bill of sale ... all legal-like ... see? Awww, no!

NOTE: For your information: Canada's gun registration program has been very controversial since day one, a good system but ineffective in reducing crime and extremely expensive, but that's my opinion.

Gun registration, just like the legal age to drink alcohol, will not solve the problems of illegal possession and use of firearms. Almost any underage kid can acquire alcohol and drink. Similarly, to get your hands on a gun illegally, and to use it seems all too easy.

Quoted excerpts as reported on The Blaze TV:

> Shocking proposed law would give sheriff
> access to the homes of gun owners
> Tuesday, Feb 19, 2013 at 1:13 PM PST
> The Blaze TV

(Glenn Beck explains a lawyer's take on it:)

"Lance Palmer, Seattle trial lawyer says to the Seattle Times, they always say we'll never go house to house to get your guns, but when you see this, you have to wonder."

The Seattle Times spoke with two Democrats who admitted the bill shows why conservatives worry about encroaching government and that the provisions in the bill needed to be eliminated:

Responding to the Newtown school massacre, the bill would ban the sale of semi-automatic weapons that use detachable ammunition magazines. Clips that contain more than 10 rounds would be illegal.

But then, with respect to the thousands of weapons like that already owned by Washington residents, the bill says this:

"In order to continue to possess an assault weapon that was legally possessed on the effective date of this section, the person possessing shall ... safely and securely store the assault weapon. The sheriff of the county may, no more than once per year, conduct an inspection to ensure compliance with this subsection."

In other words, come into homes without a warrant to poke around. Failure to comply could get you up to a year in jail.

When Reality Hits

"I'm a liberal Democrat — I've voted for only one Republican in my life," Palmer told Glenn. "But now I understand why my right-wing opponents worry about having to fight a government takeover."

He added: "It's exactly this sort of thing that drives people into the arms of the NRA (National Rifle Association)." I have been blasting the NRA for its paranoia in the gun-control debate. But Palmer is right — you can't fully blame them, when cops going door-to-door show up in legislation.

I (Glenn) spoke to two of the sponsors. One, Sen. Adam Kline, D-Seattle, a lawyer who typically is hyper-attuned to civil-liberties issues, said he did not know the bill authorized police searches because he had not read it closely before signing on.

"I made a mistake," Kline said. "I frankly should have vetted this more closely."

Glenn explained that gun prices were rising and in many places it was hard to find guns in stock. Bullets and primers that are used to make bullets are also difficult to purchase in stores due to short supplies.

Glenn Beck, The Blaze TV[28]

What is difficult for me to understand is why so many good American patriots are so quiet about the impending loss of their Second Amendment rights. Oh ... I'm sorry that hasn't happened yet? Really? Well is everyone going to wait till it is a done deal before making mass objections?

This kind of reminds me of the "Affordable Care Act" a.k.a. Obamacare, and all the promises the President made: "If you like your plan, you can keep your plan. If you like your doctor, you can keep your doctor." Over and over again, we heard it, only to finally be faced with the problems he knew about even before (and while) he was making all these promises. But the health care act, or the Obamacare law, did not get its due reaction from the public until millions of people lost their insurance plans and doctors. That woke up millions to the reality of the program!

Lately, I have been wondering if President John F Kennedy knew Barack Obama, and what Obama was up to, when he told people to 'ask what they could do for their country.'

But then I realize that the time line could be a problem, regarding the two presidents. Maybe President Obama could fix that, but I can't.

Two very different men and two very different time periods, but it won't hurt to remember what President John F Kennedy stood for in his public life.

---

28 Shocking proposed law would give sheriff access to the homes .., http://www.glennbeck.com/2013/02/19/shocking-proposed-law-would-give-sheriff-access-to-the-homes-of-gun-owners/ (accessed Feb. 20   2013)

John F. Kennedy, in his inaugural speech, said: *"Ask NOT what your country can do for you, but rather ask what YOU can do for your country."*

Was he speaking about big business practice, or was he talking to "Joe Public" about the growing attitude of entitlement that was already beginning to show up in society back then in the 1960s?

The roaring 60s. Wow, I have some trouble focusing on the .... Oh yeah, those were roaring 60s ... wow, the years when there were beatniks followed by hippies and everyone had soul-searching questions.

Yeah I'm remembering now strumming the guitar for hours on end and singing. .... But I can't play the guitar, ... maybe that didn't matter then, it just made the singing sound better. ... Yeah that's it, oh and those long nights were great, forgetting to sleep made for nice long nights, for playing and singing and solving the world's problems.

Those were the days of what's his name ... man ... D ... L.S ... D ... LS D ... LSD ... yeah ... Larry? Leary? Timothy Leary! Just as I thought, bad things also happened when we were younger. Timothy Leary claimed to have the answers ... through the use of LSD.

Mind expanding, for some, mind exploding for others, but mostly "bad trips" were the results of "finding yourself" through the use of those mind-bending, mind-numbing, mind-altering substances. Fortunately, there were the voices of reason and a strong resistance from many decent people to the use of illegal drugs.

Timothy Leary was a college professor who was a bad influence on his students, and with his blessing, the use of drugs, although already fairly widespread at the time, became an epidemic. Some of our friends were into the professor's ramblings, and got caught up in the transition from Beatnik to Hippy, and the culture of heavy drug use.

You know the mind is a great thing, a memory bank that can take you back centuries, or so it seems. A long time ago we met with some of our friends and while visiting, the subject of using drugs came up as it did quite often. Both Dave and Mike said, you can't afford not to use those drugs and miss the chance of opening your mind to wider horizons. The wives were not so adamant and we didn't continue with the conversation. My friend Mike has since died.

The last I heard about my friend Dave, was that he had left his wife and was living the "Free love life" among all kinds of rebellious individuals, and that he'd had a "mock public wedding" with some girl. He was wearing a purple velvet suit, stoned out of his mind. That is not what my nervous little friend Dave was like, or how I wanted to remember him.

Then there was the establishment fighting back with the voices of many on the anti-drug-use movement—many good, concerned citizens, parents, politicians, and church groups. One of those concerned individuals was Paul Harvey, a straight-shooting, honest radio broadcaster who gave a soul-searching speech that almost looks today like a prophecy being fulfilled.

As reported on ABC Radio Networks:
Paul Harvey's "If I Were the Devil Transcript" from 1965
Posted on November 30, 2012
by freshmannatoday

In 1965, Paul Harvey broadcasted "If I Were The Devil." I am posting the transcript of this on Fresh Manna Today. It is really amazing to realize over 47 years ago how accurately he "prophesied" the future spiritual condition of the United States. Many of his statements were considered ridiculously outlandish at that time in history. Yet, we find ourselves today...

PAUL HARVEY'S 'IF I WERE THE DEVIL' TRANSCRIPT

If I were the devil ... If I were the Prince of Darkness, I'd want to engulf the whole world in darkness. And I'd have a third of its real estate, and four-fifths of its population, but I wouldn't be happy until I had seized the ripest apple on the tree — Thee. So I'd set about however necessary to take over the United States. I'd subvert the churches first — I'd begin with a campaign of whispers. With the wisdom of a serpent, I would whisper to you as I whispered to Eve: 'Do as you please.'

"To the young, I would whisper that 'The Bible is a myth.' I would convince them that man created God instead of the other way around. I would confide that what's bad is good, and what's good is 'square.' And the old, I would teach to pray, after me, 'Our Father, which art in Washington...'

"And then I'd get organized. I'd educate authors in how to make lurid literature exciting, so that anything else would appear dull and uninteresting. I'd threaten TV with dirtier movies and vice versa. I'd pedal narcotics to whom I could. I'd sell alcohol to ladies and gentlemen of distinction. I'd tranquilize the rest with pills.

"If I were the devil I'd soon have families at war with themselves, churches at war with themselves, and nations at war with themselves; until each in its turn was consumed. And with promises of higher ratings I'd have mesmerizing media fanning the flames. If I were the devil I would encourage schools to refine young intellects, but neglect to discipline emotions — just let those run wild, until before you knew it, you'd have to have drug sniffing dogs and metal detectors at every schoolhouse door.

"Within a decade I'd have prisons overflowing, I'd have judges promoting pornography — soon I could evict God from the courthouse, then from the schoolhouse, and then from the houses of Congress. And in His own churches I would substitute psychology for religion, and deify science. I would lure priests and pastors into misusing boys and girls, and church money. If I were the devil I'd make the symbols of Easter an egg and the symbol of Christmas a bottle.

"If I were the devil I'd take from those who
have, and give to those who wanted until I
had killed the incentive of the ambitious. And
what do you bet? I could get whole states to
promote gambling as the way to get rich? I
would caution against extremes and hard work,
in Patriotism, in moral conduct. I would convince the young that marriage is old-fashioned,
that swinging is more fun, that what you see
on the TV is the way to be. And thus I could
undress you in public, and I could lure you into
bed with diseases for which there is no cure.
In other words, if I were the devil I'd just keep
right on doing what he's doing. Paul Harvey,
good day."

Paul Harvey 1965

God is good, All the time. [29]

by freshmannatoday

When I think about the media today, and how biased it
has become, I find it amazing to think that this man, Paul
Harvey—in the 1960s—was able to freely speak his mind on
issues like he did, I feel sad about the changes. What good
does it do to report news, leaving an impression that is false,
or for some reason ignoring or neglecting to tell all the facts.
Has the media become so political that, when you mention

---

29   Paul Harvey's "If I Were the Devil Transcript" from .., http://freshman-
     natoday.wordpress.com/2013/04/15/paul-harveys-if-I-were-the-devil-
     transcript-from-1965-2/ (accessed April 21   2013)

to your friends, "I saw this on *'this'* network's newscast" they look at you as if you have finally flipped your lid? There is the proof that they watch 'that' network, the poor souls.

Hey just wait you guys. What do you really know about 'this channel' and how often do you tune-in to 'that' network's newscasts?

With the way today's media is going, it will soon be impossible to get honest journalism in news reporting. When the media is so influenced by politics that trust and truth is lost, it is a very sad state of affairs for all concerned. The future may hold state-run and state-controlled media. If that happens, our socialist counterparts will be triumphant, and a dictatorship may be next on the horizon.

Believe it, it is happening here.

16. Who can we count on?

Why should we have to count or rely on anyone?

The Human race by its very nature is conditioned to be reliant on others and we get that training from day one. If left alone after birth, life will be very short, a newborn baby will not survive, crying to be fed, looked after and be loved is a very basic need that we all started life with. As we get older, that reliance is taken a step further and a whole new world opens up for us, we go to school to learn from our teachers whom we expect to have knowledge that they are willing to teach to us. The various stages of schooling become a basis for our life, a foundation that we need to build on as we continue in life.

Until that point we have been counting on our support system, home, parents, family, etc., to supply us with our basic needs such as food, clothing and shelter. Now we are at the point of becoming independent and become responsible for ourselves, and our own needs. This usually involves getting a job and starting establishing your individual life; finding a partner with whom you wish to share your life and start a family, then start the cycle all over when the babies are born.

That is normally what happens and has happened from the beginning. We are all dependent on others for the better part of our lives and that is just fine. We work together and in harmony to help each other and enjoy life.

There are forces at work that would like to change that and they have good and reasonable intentions. Our social systems are set up to help us through difficult times when we lose our job or we have an accident, are unable to work due to an illness etc., those are all very good.

As a youngster I learned that whenever you use the word "too" as in too much, there is a problem, but I also felt that too much money would not be a problem I would have to ever worry about.

Have you ever received a letter that makes you sad, angry, and happy all at the same time? It's confusing to say the least, but it requires attention so I talked to my wife. Right? I count on my wife to help me out of the messes I get myself into.

Any man would do the same—go to their wife—because women understand confusion. So I told Irene that my mother was faced with a problem. My sister and her husband and kids were moving into their own home, but now mother was faced with having to have strangers move into her home. Yes, mother could count on the local authorities to make her life miserable, with their continuing demands that she share her space.

Irene's reply was simple. "Why don't we move in with her?" More confusing emotions came flooding in. What a mess. Please understand, Irene could spend five minutes debating with herself about what brand of detergent to buy, but a decision about moving to another continent was just a snap decision to her, with no second thought required.

Yes ... I know ... I caved. I must admit that there was a certain amount of excitement that came along with the idea of travelling part way around the world. That we could buy a car there, and then travel around Europe made the idea even more interesting. And so we began preparing for the move, getting our travels planned, and selling some of our belongings. I had made a crib for our first baby, and when the second one was on the way, I had built a child's bed. We advertised a lot of things in the local paper, and were surprised at how much interest there was in what we were selling. Irene had been born in Scotland, and so, being a British subject, she wanted the children added to her passport. Unfortunately, it was still in her maiden name and the kids had her married name, like me, and so could not be added to her existing passport. To apply for a new passport, and have the kids added to it, meant filling out new application forms and new passport pictures. This was in the 1960s, and was going to take some time. My friend Mike said that he would do the passport pictures for us, to speed up the process.

The weekend was busy but I knew I could count on Mike. He came over with all his camera equipment. He set up and did a bang-up job of having Irene pose for the pictures. He took some extra shots of the kids and told us that they would be done within the week. On Tuesday morning, Mike was back before daybreak, upset that he had messed up. All his work had been done with an empty camera. Now he was back with his camera, and several rolls of film, to quickly take some shots of Irene and rush back with the film for developing and printing. When the pictures came, everything was rushed off to the British embassy for processing. Because of time constraints, we asked for a special rush to be put on the process. They were happy to oblige.

We had sold a number of items that were being picked up, and so we prepared the crib and the bed for the new owners. As I had built them in the bedroom, there ended up being a problem with the size of the doors. They were just not big enough to allow the bed to leave. Always enjoying a challenge, I figured out that we could take the bed out through the window, if we removed the glass. Luckily it was a sliding window. The bed would just fit through the empty frame. Happy with the outcome of the situation, I stepped back to admire my accomplishment, and promptly broke the sliding glass window. "Aw … now what have I done?" It was a good thing we were paid well for the crib and the bed!

We now had to move into a motel for a while before our departure. The motel was fine and we were quite comfortable, but once I sold the car, it made things a bit difficult in terms of getting around. Our friend Mike lent me his truck. Finally the day of our departure arrived. We had said our goodbyes at work and to our friends, but we still had no passport for Irene. Our travel agent, Bud, had telexed the British embassy, telling them that it had not come yet. In desperation, he phoned the embassy and made arrangements to have the passport delivered to the train station in Ottawa, which we would eventually come to on our way across Canada. Good man, that Bud.

Our local train station, from which we would be starting our journey, was about seven miles out of town, and Bud had promised to take us there: Irene, myself, the two babies, plus seventeen pieces of choice luggage. The train was on time at two thirty in the morning. We said goodbye to Bud, and were escorted to our bedroom compartment for the trip across the country—without most of our luggage. We could not keep our luggage in the bedroom compartment if we wanted to sleep in our beds, so the luggage went into a storage compartment. The bedroom compartment resembled a glove compartment of a 1960s car in size.

Train travel was nothing new to me, having travelled to work by commuter train before, but this train was definitely different. There was a dining car, an observation car with a raised deck, and some bedroom and sleeper cars. We settled in for the night and I began to realize what we had done. Reality hit! "Ooh you nut case! You are headed for disaster and taking Irene and the kids along with you! Well, you better make the best of it now!

When we got to Winnipeg, I knew that the train would be stopped for some time. It looked so nice and sunny that I decided to go and make some telephone calls to some old friends. As soon as I stepped out of the train I just about died from the extreme cold. A coat would have been appropriate dress for that time of the year in Winnipeg. On the phone, I caught up on some news and whatever current issues my friends were having. After sharing for a while, I went back outside to the train ... just in time to see it moving away. The face of a panicked Irene looked out at me from the window of our compartment, as the train left without me. I waved at her, and then the train stopped. Luckily, the train had just been moved to make repairs to one of the cars. Apparently there had been a derailment the night before, causing some damage. You can miss so much excitement when you're fast asleep.

North America looks big on the map, but when you are travelling by train from west to east you begin to realize just how big it really is. You travel for days and nights at breakneck speed and realize that you've only gone a few inches on the map. It's awesome! We wondered when we would arrive in Ottawa. The answer came while we were fast asleep. There was some knocking on the bedroom door that woke us up. In my underwear, I stumbled to the door, and there he was: a right proper Englishman, dressed in tails, wearing a bowler hat, and carrying an umbrella. With his mac over his arm, he introduced himself and asked my name. Next, this gentleman handed me a brand new passport for Irene. "With the compliments of Her Majesty." He said goodbye then, and disappeared into the deep cold night. This was a government we could count on. It was too bad it was across the North Atlantic.

We need to be able to count on our politicians to look after us when it comes to government matters, and in a democratic system, it is supposed to work by having two or more parties looking out for our well being, and the good of the country. Government spending is usually considered a necessary evil, but without it we wouldn't have roads, water, sewers, or an infrastructure to supply the many other basic needs of a country. You have got to be able to count on your government to provide and maintain the services at every level of government.

The three levels of government each have responsibilities for looking after the basics, and therefore, they each levy taxes to provide for those services. Today however, we're faced with an entitlement mentality that shows up in too many areas of our society. The costs of the overwhelming demands for entitlements are much greater than what the tax revenues can provide.

The businessman talks about increasing the supply (product) to meet the demand.

In government, the politicians should be talking about, decreasing the demands based on the supply (taxes).

When we, as a society, begin to look to the government to provide us with all of our needs, and start expecting everything to be provided and paid for by the government, we may feel entitled to have it as our right. Expecting to be paid when not working, receiving unemployment or welfare benefits, food stamps, and other such sources of income, leads to poverty. The social welfare system is supposed to be used for extreme cases, when no other source of income is possible. It will pay for housing, medical, and dental, plus living expenses ... while taking away our dignity.

We create a society of entitlement, one without dignity, when we take no responsibility for the way we live. When we are not looking after our own families and after ourselves, then the government is completely in charge and we eventually lose all our rights. The scary part of that sort of development is that we could lose our freedom of speech, our freedom of religion, our rights: to vote, to look after our parents, to look after our children and their education, healthcare and so on.

Oh sure, you say how can I believe all that stuff about the government taking my rights away, we live in a free country! We are the citizens of a free country and our fathers and grandfathers, even our brothers and sisters, have put their lives on the line and fought for our freedom. Surely I will be able to look after my kids and my family?

Well I hope you can remember that as you enter the fight to keep that freedom, just remember: "if you like your doctor you can keep your doctor" and "if you like your plan you can keep your plan;" those were promises made by the president of the US; did you believe him when he said that? Maybe don't believe everything you hear, check it out!

So check this out: A 15 year old girl being treated for a serious disease is taken from her parents' care and placed into the custody of the State of Massachusetts. The girl, Justina Pelletier from West Hartford, Connecticut was a normal teenager that loved figure skating and many other activities that teens enjoy. When she became ill, her parents took her to Tufts Medical Centre in Boston where her doctors diagnosed and treated her for mitochondrial disorder for about a year.

In February, 2012, she was taken to a second hospital in Boston, Massachusetts, as one of her doctors had transferred there. The doctors she saw quickly determined that the diagnosis was wrong (according to them) and that she suffered from psychiatric problems. They didn't continue with the medical treatment for mitochondrial disorder. When the Pelletiers wanted Justina discharged to take her back to the original Tufts hospital, also in Boston and then to their home in Connecticut, they were refused and charged with medical child abuse. In February, 2013, Justina Pelletier was officially placed in permanent custody of the Department of Children and Families of the state of Massachusetts.

During her confinement in the Boston hospital she has not received her needed medical treatment, education or access to religious services. Most jails or prisons are better to their inmates and provide them with what they need.

Who would ever expect this from a children's hospital?

The Pelletier family has had an ongoing fight to get their teen home to Connecticut where she would be getting treatment for the diagnosed mitochondrial disorder. This is a fight that may be ongoing for some time, but what about Justina, will she survive this ordeal and the family, how much else can they endure?

In a news item just released, we were told that Justina's case has had a lot of exposure in the press after Lou Pelletier broke a court imposed gag order. She is being released to Tufts Medical Centre where she will be receiving the proper medical care she needs. Hopefully Justina's weakened condition is such that with the proper care she may recover from this ordeal and her illness.

Lou Pelletier and his lawyer were cautiously optimistic; they know the wheels of justice or rather the law turn slowly, who knows how long it will take before the hospital will act on this court decision; she needs to be looked after NOW!

Entitlements are frequently referred to in our society, and many people seem to have the idea that the government can spend tax money for whatever it wishes. Those same people believe that they are entitled to so many things, and want it in order to get their fair share. The government spending is often greater than the revenue from our taxes, unfortunately, many politicians also feel that the government can spend freely—often without concern for overspending!

A number of years ago we hired a new immigrant based on his qualifications; he came to work for us as a draughtsman and his work seemed okay. As I got to know him a bit better he surprised me with his knowledge, not general knowledge but specific knowledge about all the social services and *his* rights. He knew the government departments, the free handouts by the government and all the things he was now entitled to since he had moved to Canada... Since you asked, yes of course he brought his wife and kids too. What amazed me was his in-depth knowledge of all the entitlements within a year, of which I, after some thirty-five years was totally unaware and clueless.

Some time later while I was living in Washington, my wife sent me a newspaper article.

Still in disbelief, I remember reading this article some time ago about a person who was speeding and got stopped by the police, was awarded with a fine for speeding but had a defence, he was late for a job interview. The police was unimpressed and gave the ticket anyway. Not willing to pay, this went to court and the poor driver who was unemployed and on welfare was now also faced with a fine. The court heard the case about having to rush and drive his car at high speeds, because he was late for a job interview. The judge hearing this case actually found for the defendant, this poor unemployed welfare recipient that didn't get up in time for his job interview got off.

Although some time ago now, I also remember a time when our courts were called "Court of Justice" but now they are usually called "Court of Law" no longer Justice, doesn't that imply something?

This creates chaos and I don't mean KAOS, the evil agency that agents 86 and 99 were fighting in Get Smart. Those TV characters showed off some good things at "Control", their agency's headquarters, by using the "Cone of Silence." I think that's something the present US Administration may take notice of.

Governments that lose sight of a balanced approach in governing, forget that almost anything "out of balance" creates chaos, and chaos makes for trouble in almost every area of life— including government spending. When chaos occurs, people look to their leaders to sort things out. This becomes an even bigger problem when those very same government leaders are the ones responsible for creating the chaos in the first place.

The answer is not; to spend too much money, then raise the taxes. It is not; to raise the taxes and then lose more jobs. Losing more jobs raises the numbers of people on unemployment, or receiving welfare and food stamps. If there is not enough money to pay for unemployment, welfare, and food stamps, the answer is not to raise the taxes once again. Raising the taxes again loses more jobs. Losing more jobs raises the numbers of people on unemployment, or receiving welfare and food stamps ... and so on, and so on ...

The proverbial vicious circle eventually spins totally out of control, much like the spinning cycle in a washing machine. If the clothes in the washing machine are not balanced, we know that the machine will start bouncing around and even stop altogether, unless we bring the clothing in the machine back into balance.

Creating a balance is a very important principle in every aspect of life. Working for a living is an important part of life. However, living within our means is equally important in order to have a balanced life. For many families in recent years (and in the present), this is a hard lesson to learn. Recently, the redistribution of wealth has been the topic of many conversations. It is a principle of socialism, but wealth is often misunderstood. Wealth consists of assets minus liabilities. In other words, when you subtract the amount of money an individual owes (their liabilities), from the value of their belongings (their assets — things like houses and cars), you establish their actual wealth. Income is what is earned, or any source of financial gains.

Responsible government's spending = TAXES (income) — (debt + liabilities) = Balanced budget

Government's irresponsible spending = TAXES (income) — (debt + interest + liabilities) = DEBT

The politicians should be talking about and working on decreasing the demand of the entitlements, based on the supply of available tax money as allotted in the budget. **No** fiscal budget should be driven by entitlements.

Recently a young lady got quite a bit of attention by fighting for the cost of contraceptives to be covered by the Obamacare law/insurance debacle. She claimed as a university student that contraceptive expenses were a burden to students and that $3,000.- per year added to the costs of tuition makes it too difficult for students. My reaction was, what was she studying if she spent $3,000.- per year on contraceptives, that is more than $8.- per day, how does she get the time to attend classes and study in addition to all that extra curricular activity.

She must have made her point very well because it now is another entitlement included in Obamacare. This would make a good case for prostitutes to have all of their required tools of the trade paid for by Obamacare, the Affordable Care Act.

The entitlement ideas are a result of socialist ideologies, and although all of socialism is not totally wrong in practice, the problems tend to become greater and may fail to live up to what is pictured. With the socialist and communist ideologies, the danger exists that the leadership turns into a dictatorship, which usually loses sight of the people's wellbeing. A dictatorship would be a terrible thing for today's Americans and would totally destroy what is left of American life today.

Who or what can you rely on. The answer will be "DEATH and TAXES," but entitlement, forget it!

An entitlement society is unsustainable.

Don't rely on the government but put your trust in God.

17. Summary

In the previous chapters, I've described (in my own clumsy way) about the good, the bad, and the ugly things in life. I've tried to be honest in my perception of what I have experienced, witnessed, researched, and now foresee as to what is ahead of us—some of which has already started. Not being a prophet, I hope that the future will not be as bad as it appears to me.

War. It is hell while the fight is on, but even when we're told it's over, and the fighting is done, it is not over ... for many it is *never* over. How do you recover from war? How does one get over the decisions that are necessary in a combat situation? It's you or me ... and I can see you're scared, but so am I ... so who dies first? How do you get over sending someone on a mission that you know they might not come back from? How do you shake the fear? How do you deal with the nightmares and the feelings of guilt?

It's nice to know that there are organizations that are in the business of helping people get through the rough spots, but most veterans who have seen active duty and engaged in combat are scarred for life. Most cities that have suffered during a war will carry the physical scars for years ... but when repairs and rebuilding are complete, the damage that was most obvious is no longer visible. We humans are not so easily fixed; we tend to carry the scars a lot longer. We seem to heal, over time, but the deep scars remain.

After the fighting wars came the "Cold War". No military fights this time, just politicians doing what they do best: talking a lot, creating tension, and not accomplishing much else at all. The atomic bomb was a real threat for many European and other countries. Next, the hydrogen bomb appeared on the scene, and that caused even more concern. While all of this was going on, the Korean War came about, and in order to keep the communists out of South Korea, this military war was anything but cold. The Korean War lasted almost three years (1950-1953). North and South Korea are still not united today.

The Korean War was followed by the Vietnam War, which was fought very differently. It quickly became apparent that this war would not bring a resounding victory. Many Vietnam veterans were totally discouraged about the way the war ended. The Vietnam War actually lasted from 1955-1975, but the US was only involved from 1960 until1973, at which time the troops were pulled out.

There were wars in Europe's communist block countries and the Middle East, and all around there has been political unrest and tensions, giving us lots of reasons for concern. Then the Berlin wall came down. That eased tensions a lot. But then the economic situations added to the concerns.

Since September 11, 2001, the war on terrorism has been a serious conflict. It is yet another type of warfare with an enemy that is elusive and mostly faceless—they are not known as identifiable, uniformed soldiers but are blended in with the rest of the citizens instead. With sleeper cells all around the world, and nearly impossible to identify, you may have a terrorist living next door or in the same building you're living in. The unknown brings no particular comfort to us, but creates a distrust of anyone we don't know very well.

The Gulf War was a precursor to the Iraq War. The war in Afghanistan, and Libya both had to do with terrorism, even though they are 'not terrorists. No Sir. They are just bad boys. The politically correct term is "violent extremists."

All these wars had victims on the battlefield, and survivors who have to deal with the trauma of what they have gone through. The mental and physical damage seems to become more severe with each involvement. It appears that the international conflicts, wars and rumours of war, are constantly on the news—not leaving much time for recovery.

What happened to the United Nations? Weren't they supposed to prevent war? Was that not part of the deal? No war, just peaceful coexistence, that was the goal of the UN—just the type of referee that is needed when there are differences of opinion.

The UN showed its true colours with the forming of the World Health Organization, and again with Agenda 21. When it came to the war on terrorism though, they welcomed the NATO organization with open arms—allowing it to do the dirty work.

The discussion on the rights of the elderly, and euthanasia, makes me feel that, as part of the UN functions, there is a strong desire for population control. Then, when it gets involved in discussions on gay rights, it makes me even more upset, as that is (again) not part of the UN's function.

All Member States must obey the Charter and Countries must try to settle their differences by peaceful means.

- Member Countries must avoid using force or threatening to use force.

- The UN **may not interfere** in the domestic affairs of any country.

- All member Countries are encouraged to try to assist the United Nations.

It just keeps getting worse, and that bothers me a lot. For instance, the UN promotes and uses redistribution of wealth in a number of ways. We are already subjected to that by our own governments, and really don't need the UN adding to it. There are many additional taxes planned; if and when they come, we will be taxed to provide for charity purposes (entitlements). Or could it be for destruction of our society? We know that, by using executive power order, President Obama ignores the Constitution of the United States of America, and that more restrictions will be imposed.

There is (and should be) a real fear of the UN and of a government that goes along with everything the UN comes up with. There is a real danger that the powers that are at work in the UN could become The New World Order.

Remember, Paul Harvey and his speech: "If I Were the Devil". It seems almost prophetic today —to our shame.

As we talked about wartime and the good life before and after the Second World War, I didn't talk about the fact that, during the Second World War, the churches started to fill up and people turned to God for help. Veterans have told me that some of the most sincere and urgent prayers were voiced in the trenches. For quite some time, churches were places of refuge for many survivors of the war. Gradually, as the good life returned, so did the feeling of self-sufficiency. In the seventies and eighties, there was a falling away from church life again. Successful and independent, a lot of people (feeling self-sufficient) lost the need for dependence on God.

There are several influences that come into play in today's confusing and complicated world: economic and political problems that are constantly facing us; a strong and growing Muslim population that has an influence on today's religious community; and an ever-growing socialist ideology putting even more pressure on us all. Let's take a look at all these things—just to make sure that we understand each other.

The economy is a problem that appears to be widespread, and is not just a local issue. Any country or territory will have a local economy, which will fluctuate to some extent. It is usually connected to a wider area though, and a greater or global economy. America used to have a very big, strong economy that could be manipulated (to some extent) from within, but having become deeply indebted to outside sources, this kind of manipulation is no longer as effective. A healthy economy has a strong manufacturing, export, and import base to keep balance. This will also keep employment at a healthy level. An economy that is completely reliant on the export of its natural resources—lumber, ore, and oil, for example—is dependent on the export market demands, and may not be sustainable. When an economy is based largely on tourism, the fluctuations in the global economy will have an immediate effect that can be devastating.

With the constant population growth and immigration, legal and illegal, comes an influx of people from other countries, cultures, ideologies, and religions. While there are obviously exceptions to every rule, and no race or ethnicity can be painted with a single brush, there are trends and patterns that can be observed. The Latino population is growing, and generally displays an intense desire to fit into the local culture and economy. The Middle Eastern population tends to congregate and stay more within its own community, which makes integration into local culture and society much more difficult. The Asian population is similar, but tends to blend into the local economy and life better. African immigrants are usually very eager to fit in and are industrious and anxious to make a living, learning as much as possible about what goes on around them. As for the Europeans, they seem a lot like the Latino group, settling down with a desire to blend in and be involved with the local community.

Since September 11, 2001, we suddenly became more aware of the Muslim families. More of the women in those families, who had kept mainly to themselves and wearing normal western clothing, were now easily identified by their Muslim headdresses, and the longer dresses. This was our observation, however this may not have been the case everywhere in North America. For me, it brought mixed emotions. It was intriguing to see that they identified with a religion, but upsetting that September 11th seemed to be an event signalling them to come out of the closet. Most Latino, Asian, African, and European people also have a religion and have practised that religion openly. After all, there is freedom of religion here. Well ... for now.

There are two societal pressures that appear to increase as time goes by:

1. The pressure on governments to add to the already financially crippling entitlements, which are an underlying problem caused by socialism. When taxes are spent irresponsibly, and our governments just keep adding to their debts, it comes back to haunt us our children, our grandchildren, and our great-grand children!

2. The increasing demands of the vocal Muslims to change our society to fit their laws and customs. It constantly amazes me that they want to change the laws of our land, to Sharia law, and expect us to make changes for them within our school system, where we cannot even retain our own long established customs—our own prayers having been banned.

It must be apparent that our ups and downs are influenced by the economic and political conditions of the countries in which we live. If we lose the sovereignty of our nation, and become burdened by a ruling entity without the values we hold dear, our freedom will be lost, along with any hope of ever being the proud nations we once were. Already we have lost our freedom of speech to some extent. They have been restricted by our political leanings. When it comes to the use of the word "terrorist" or "God," or being allowed to pray in our public schools, or singing Christmas carols, we have to show political correctness. Whatever happened to separation of state and church? If the state represents politics, then shouldn't we leave church and religion out of the equation?

Our freedom to travel is already hampered as well, because of terrorist activity and suspect behaviour around the world.

Having an extra few hours to spend at the Los Angeles Airport (sequestered while a squad team did their work) was annoying, but arriving safely at the intended destination was great! Having San Francisco Airport Security, with their guns at the ready, behind my wife while I stood on my stocking feet was embarrassing, but once my shoes were checked out and my luggage was checked again, everything was okay. My pride was hurt, but we again arrived safely at our destination. It is very important that airport security take their work seriously, and when they become too relaxed, it really gives us reason for concern. Our freedom to travel to other countries is somewhat restricted now, compared to before September 11, 2001, but with some document preparation, we can still go almost anywhere we want to travel.

Next, losing the second amendment rights is, for true Americans, a devastating loss, as the constitution has provided for these rights—rights that only the ideologies of socialists and communists try to take away.

Text of the 2nd Amendment to the Constitution of the US:

A well regulated Militia, being necessary to the security of a free State, the right of the people to keep and bear Arms, shall not be infringed. [30]

We have had tremendous changes in technology and the way our economy is stimulated; we have seen the political

---

30 2nd Amendment -Text of the 2nd Amendment, http://americanhistory. about.com/od/usconstitution/a/2nd-Amendment.htm (accessed May 18 2013)

landscape evolve to the point where a campaign full of empty promises and backed by lots of money will buy a winner. We have seen government corruption take place without the accountability promised by the same administration. Now we are faced with the consequences in our own near future. The next generations will also suffer from our apathy.

We looked at the organizations that were created to resolve conflicts and prevent wars from happening. We saw that the intents and purposes of these organizations have changed dramatically, to a point of great concern. We have witnessed the results of radical ideologies turning people into terrorists. The educational system's deterioration has allowed our colleges and universities to promote and teach very liberal ideologies, while ignoring critical-thinking processes.

Apathy in politics becomes a problem of our own making:

- Wars are the result of intolerance and poor politics.

- Terrorism is the result of intolerance and hatred, mostly from outside influences.

- Entitlement is the result of creating dependence and poor governance.

- Overspending by governments creates dependence on lenders, mostly from outside sources.

All these things are NOT sustainable.

Where is all this going and what will the future bring? If in fact we are losing control of our own country and our own politicians, as well as the responsibility of raising our kids (as it becomes a community responsibility), and if we are being subjected to ideologies with which we are in conflict, then the end of life as intended may be near.

Just to review what we talked about in the various chapters:

With just a glimpse we covered the good life in the thirties, those days were waning just before and during the great depression. A strange phenomenon that occurred was the dumping of many tons of cheap Asian products on the European markets.

Many people had not seen the good life for years and now the world was in turmoil, war breaking out everywhere. The Second World War was havoc, insecure masses were thrown into conflicts that they had little or nothing to do with, but were drawn into regardless. Pain and suffering were all around and life seemed even more fragile.

Next came the restoration, the rebuilding of lives and buildings and infrastructure, wow a very big task but it needed doing and was accomplished over time. With all this activity, the economy started to pick up and after some ten years, things were looking pretty good again. With that there was a slow return to the good life.

Well I must admit it was terrific to be able to live the good life and in North America we know how to enjoy it. Of course being comfortable does not mean you stay alert and soon the dreaded Apathy starts to take hold in our lives again. We must learn to deal with it.

The beatniks and the hippies had their own ideas like 'make love not war' which of course prevented the war in Vietnam, … no? … hey … man, do you mean there was a war in Vietnam? Oh wow! And all I wanted was peace, no more wars, just peace, like world peace?

Most of us want peace in the world, but at this point we have to start looking at what is next, euthanasia and cloning, I hope that they got your attention because they are ideas that are becoming a reality. When certain groups are pushing to take your life it becomes personal and when they are thinking of making a copy of you or me it becomes objectionable, brrrr.

Just when you think about taking it easy, like in retirement, there is a need for you to become involved on the school board, I mean it, become a school board trustee so you can be like the professional sportsmen and stand up for what you believe in, like bringing prayer back to the school, to the classroom.

Yes, we have been fighting wars for the freedom of others and yes, those were very noble deeds, but now it is time we stay alert so that we don't lose our own freedom due to apathy, it could be our own enemy.

If at all possible, we must avoid war altogether, war is Hell.

We have had some depression and some recession recently and slowly we're *not* recovering as quickly as we should. Of course the world economy has been in the dumpster for a while and the Asian countries are dumping tons of goods on our markets daily, yes sir just like before the Second World War, but we are okay, right?

Have you noticed the violent attacks around the world and in the US, is it me or are people going nuts? What do you think about my asking all these questions, it is probably politically incorrect?

Hmm … maybe not if I add 'Have a nice day eh?'

You know that 'Fair trade' is a great way to help the less fortunate in other countries and balance the scales in international commerce, something that has been a long time coming.

But what about the scare of Global Warming, if you ask Al Gore, he will have us growing coconuts at the North Pole fairly soon; a lot of scientist don't agree with him but then remember, they are not ex-vice presidents nor did they invent the internet.

Things are heating up, no doubt changes are needed before it is too late; the US administration is taking the country in the wrong direction and into ruin. The respect that was once almost unique to the US around the world is gone, and the president has lost his credibility with the people.

Let your voice be heard when election time rolls around, vote for what and who you believe in. Don't believe or rely on entitlements or false promises. Vote, vote! It's your right and your duty.

The Bible is clear about wars and rumours of war. Has that any meaning for you? Or are suggestions of the end times what makes you shrug your shoulders and walk away? Have you serious questions about your future and what it will mean to you? Is the end really the end ... or is there life after death?

Although I am not a preacher or a prophet, I have the assurance of having a future now and after ... because Jesus paid my ransom. He paid the price.

Sure, I know that we must prepare for our future and that retirement is part of that. Also important for now and the future is being prepared for natural disasters. When I see all the advertisements for survival equipment and survival foods it makes me acutely aware that there are imminent dangers that we may not be able to prepare for. All that is true! There are dangers looming with a group like the UN bent on controlling our lives and the world, as well as terrorist Muslims desiring to convert or kill everyone. These are real dangers, but you know as scary as that is, I try not to worry about that.

What I am concerned about is the fact that people are dying all around us every day, and they haven't prepared for their future. And I am concerned about the fact that I haven't told all the people around me that my future is secure and that their lives may also be secure. I've missed so many opportunities to tell my friends and people I meet about the GOD who loves them. You must know that there is life after death, and you can have a future because JESUS also paid your ransom, HE paid the price.

A very old Prophecy

But you must realize that in the last days the times will be full of danger. Men will become utterly self-centered, greedy for money, full of big words. They will be proud and contemptuous, without any regard for what their parents taught them. They will be utterly lacking in gratitude, purity and normal human affections. They will be men of unscrupulous speech and have no control of themselves. They will be passionate and unprincipled, treacherous, self-willed and conceited, loving all the time what gives them pleasure instead of loving God. They will maintain a façade of religion but their conduct will deny its validity. You must keep clear of people like this. [31] — Second Timothy 3: 1-5

---

31 Second Timothy 3: 1-5

It is my sincere pleasure and privilege to know that you were reading this book, a book with a lot of talk about war and peace, and organizations promising world peace, while our world is struggling for that elusive ideal! My prayer is that you will have a desire to have personal peace in your life, while there is so little peace around us. Knowing the inner peace that only God can give is what makes it possible to continue with life in those difficult days. When you do desire that peace, pray that Jesus, the Son of God, will forgive your sins and receive you into his family.

Arthur Berm

18. Citations

INTRODUCTION

Glenn Beck and Harriet Parke, AGENDA 21, New York, Threshold Editions/Mercury Radio arts, a Division of Simon & Schuster, Inc. 2012

Chapter 1

2   Marshall Plan-Wikipedia, the free encyclopedia, http://en.wikipedia.org/wiki/marshall_plan/ (accessed February 5, 2014)

Chapter 2

  - None -

Chapter 3

3   Franklin, Access to the FDR Library's Digital Collections, www.FDRlibrary.marist.edu/archives/collections/franklin/(accessed Jan. 28, 2013)

4   League of Nations — Wikipedia, the free encyclopedia, http://en. Wikipedia..org./wikw/legue_of_nations/(accessed Jan. 13 2013)

5   United Nations, Wikipedia, the free encyclopedia, http://en.wikipedia.org/wiki/unitednations/ (accessed Jan. 13 2013)

6   Lyrics from "Oh! It's a lovely war." J.P. Long and Maurice Scott, 1917

7   NATO — Wikipedia, the free encyclopedia, http://en.wikipedia.org/wiki/NATO (accessed Jan. 13 2013)

8   NATO — Wikipedia, the free encyclopedia, http://en.wikipedia.org/wiki/NATO (accessed Jan. 13 2013)

9   Tear down this wall! -Wikipedia, the free encyclopedia, http://en.wikipedia.org/wiki/tear_down_this_wall/ (accessed Feb. 10 2013)

10   Ronald Reagan Presidential Foundation & Library; NATO — Wikipedia, the free encyclopedia, http://en.wikipedia.org/wiki/NATO (accessed Feb. 10 2013)

Chapter 4

11   U.N. proposes euthanasia as right to health (it was only a.., http://www.freerepublic.com/focus/f-news/2791827/posts/U.N.-proposes-euthanasia-as-right-to-health-(it-was-only-a-matter-of-time)/ (accessed Sep. 19 2012)

12   U.N. proposes euthanasia as right to health,http://OneNewsNow.com/culture/2011/10/11/un-proposes-euthanasia-as-right-to-health (accessed Sept.19 2012)

Chapter 5

13   Genetic engineering in agriculture and the environment.., http://business.highbeam.com/411908/article-1g1-18826502/genetic-engineering-agriculture-and-environment-assessing (accessed Mar. 15 2013)

Chapter 6

14   The Stunning 355-Page Mega Report That Reveals the Radical.., http://www.theblaze.com/stories/2013/04/08/

the-stunning-355-page-mega-reportpthat-reveals-the-
radical-curriculum-at-one-american-college-and-how-a-golf-
game-gone-awry-led-to-it-all. (accessed Aug. 055 2013)

Chapter 7
15   Protesters oppose Muslim prayer in public
schools | Toronto Star, http://www.thestar.com/life/
parent/2011/07/25/protesters_oppose_muslim_
prayer_in_public_schools/html (accessed Sept. 20 2012)
16   Muslim prayer room opens in Catholic high
school | Ontario .., http://www.torontosun.
com/2012/09/17/muslim-prayer-room-opens-in-
catholic-high-school (accessed Sept. 20 2012)

Chapter 8
17   Talk:United States Bill of Rights — Wikisource,
the free .., http://en.wikisource.org/wiki/Talk:United_
STates_Bill_of_Rights (accessed May 18 2013)
18   Shocking proposed law would give sheriff access to
the homes, http://www.glennbeck.com/2013/02/19/
shocking-porposed-law-would-give-sheriff-access-to-
the-homes-of-gun-owners/ (accessed Feb. 20 2013)
19   Mathew 24:6

Chapter 9
  - None -

Chapter 10
20   Nora Fogarty — (recorded Live from 'The Factory,'
Nightclub .., http://vimeo.com/69579183 (accessed July 18 2013)

21   September 11 attacks — Wikipedia, the
free encyclopedia, http://en.wikipedia.org/wiki/
September_11_attacks (accessed July10 2013)
22   Benghazi Attack — Wikipedia, the free encyclopedia, http://en.wikipedia.org/wiki/2012_
Benghazi_attack (accessed July 12 2013)

Chapter 11

23   Same Sex Marriage — Wikipedia, the free
encyclopedia, http://en.wikipedia.org/wiki/
Same-sex marriage (accessed May 15 2013)
24   Boy Scouts' sexual orientation –
CNN.com Jan. 28 2013/The Blaze TV Jan.
28 2013 (accessed Jan. 28 2013)

Chapter 12

- None -

Chapter 13

25   Climate Talks or Wealth Redistribution Talks? | The
Foundry.., http://Blog.heritage.org/2010/11/19/climate-
talks-or-wealth-redistribution-talks/ (accessed July 18 2013)
26   Tom Gross: The UN's willful ignorance of modern-
day slavery.., http://beforeitsnews.com/eu/2013/02/
tom-gross-the-uns-willful-ignorance-of-modern-day-
slavery-2510036.html (accessed July 20 2013)
27   The Global- Warming Deception: How a
Secret Elite Plans to Bankrupt America ...
Grant R. Jeffrey (by permission from Water
Brook Press/Penguin Random House)

Chapter 14

- None -

Chapter 15

28   Shocking proposed law would give sheriff access to the homes .., http://www.glennbeck.com/2013/02/19/shocking-proposed-law-would-give-sheriff-access-to-the-homes-of-gun-owners/ (accessed_Feb. 20 2013)

29   Paul Harvey's "If I Were the Devil Transcript" from .., http://freshmannatoday.wordpress.com/2013/04/15/paul-harveys-if-I-were-the-devil-transcript-   from-1965-2/ (accessed April 21 2013)

Chapter 16

- None -

Chapter 17

30   2nd Amendment -Text of the 2nd Amendment, http://americanhistory.about.com/od/usconstitution/a/2nd-Amendment.htm (accessed May 18 2013)

31   Second Timothy 3: 1-5

In memory of Kelly Patric Doig

July 15 1959 — Sept. 2 2013

We got to know Kelly when Irene attended a training course at the Brannen Lake "playschool" where Kelly was incarcerated. The course was called "Breaking Barriers" and I think that Kelly should have been teaching the course, because he was so good at that, and at making friends. Kelly would actually introduce Irene to people as a fellow inmate, at Brannen Lake for tax evasion.

At the end of the course, a Friday evening "pizza and a movie" became a sort of tradition at the "playschool." Killer Kelly, as he was introduced to me, was anything but a killer. He was a gentle, kind fellow with a big heart. You just couldn't help but like him.

The "Breaking Barriers" course was part of a ministry to the inmates at Brannen Lake, and Kelly was very responsive to Irene, and also to the Gospel. After some time, when Kelly was ready, Irene had the privilege of leading Kelly to Jesus Christ and the forgiveness of sins.

Over the years that Kelly stayed with us, we helped him with a little landscaping business, and another of Kelly's friends, Phil Wright, joined him. As the business was growing so did the interest of other friends, and dirty Dougy came in as the spoiler. He pulled Phil, who died some time later, down. Somewhat discouraged about it all, Kelly continued on his own, working hard until the fall and winter season slowed the work down to a stop. He did snow clearing, but we got very little snow.

Did I say snow? Well, that just told us that it was a good time to go to Mexico. Puerto Vallarta here we come! We had a good time. We had such a fine vacation that we repeated it again and again. San Jose del Cabo and LaPenita have just never been the same. Spending two weeks at a time in the sun meant that Kelly used a lot of baby oil, and spent many nights in the shower.

A friend got Kelly set up with an apprenticeship program for pipe fitting, and that seemed a good opportunity. However, it meant he had to go to Saskatchewan. What happened next landed him, for the first time, in federal prison.

Life is full of opportunities and we make choices. Some are good, others aren't, but that's life. Kelly was good at getting jobs. His job at Future Shop lasted four years and was great. He was the first employee of the month in that location.

We missed Kelly after his move from our island, but he would be in touch from time to time. We are so glad that he made his peace with God and rededicated his life before passing away.

We'll miss him, but be encouraged.

Kelly is in a better place, without pain or sorrow.

CPSIA information can be obtained at www.ICGtesting.com
Printed in the USA
LVOW08s2244170714

394481LV00005B/20/P

9 781460 235836